T0146403

Praise for
Flying by the Seat of My Pants

"As a frequent flier who has accumulated enough air miles that the pilots often come ask me for directions midflight, I am very aware of the funny (as well as the not-so-funny) things that can happen to any passenger! Marsha's book gives us a behind-the-scenes look. This is a fun and honest read that humorously helps put life into perspective."

—BRAD STINE, comedian and author

"Few of us get to realize our dreams. Fewer still write about the experience. And truly rare are those who do so as captivatingly as Marsha Marks has done in *Flying By the Seat of My Pants,* by sharing a personal look at her life in the air and on the ground."

—DAVID M. ROWELL, publisher of *The Travel Insider* newsletter and Web site

"Marsha Marks is witty, entertaining, insightful, and basically herself. Her writings are a breath of fresh air."

—JOHN L. HOH JR., author of *Silent Meditations for a Silent Night*

"Laugh out loud funny. Marsha Marks gives an outstanding voice, sense of humor, and personality to the folks so many of us know only as, 'Excuse me, Miss!'"

—SUSAN FARREN, inspirational speaker
and author of *The Fireman's Wife*

"*Flying by the Seat of My Pants* is that rare sort of book that has me giggling helplessly. Marsha Marks is a winning combination of wacky class clown and quietly perceptive observer. You will *love* this ride!"

—SHAUNTI FELDHAHN, author of *For Women
Only: What You Need to Know About the
Inner Lives of Men*

"*Flying by the Seat of My Pants* is laughter at thirty-thousand feet."

—JOYCE DIXON, *Southern Scribe*

Flying by the Seat of My Pants

Flying by the Seat of My Pants

FLIGHT ATTENDANT ADVENTURES ON A WING AND A PRAYER

Marsha Marks

WATERBROOK
PRESS

FLYING BY THE SEAT OF MY PANTS
PUBLISHED BY WATERBROOK PRESS
12265 Oracle Boulevard, Suite 200
Colorado Springs, Colorado 80921

All Scripture quotations or paraphrases are taken from the *Holy Bible, New International Version*®. NIV®. Copyright © 1973, 1978, 1984 by International Bible Society. Used by permission of Zondervan Publishing House. All rights reserved. These are Psalm 23:1 (page 16), Psalm 100:3 (page 16), Matthew 10:16 (page 19), and Proverbs 3:5-6 (page 54).

ISBN 978-1-57856-699-0

Copyright © 2005 by Marsha Marks

Published in association with Yates & Yates, LLP, Attorneys and Counselors, Orange, California.

All rights reserved. No part of this book may be reproduced or transmitted in any form or by any means, electronic or mechanical, including photocopying and recording, or by any information storage and retrieval system, without permission in writing from the publisher.

Published in the United States by WaterBrook Multnomah, an imprint of the Crown Publishing Group, a division of Random House Inc., New York.

Library of Congress Cataloging-in-Publication Data
Marks, Marsha.
    Flying by the seat of my pants : flight attendant adventures on a wing and a prayer / Marsha Marks.— 1st ed.
        p. cm.
    ISBN 978-1-57856-699-0
    1. Christian life—Anecdotes. I. Title.
    BV4501.3.M267 2005
    242—dc22

                                                                2004029441

This book is dedicated to anyone who has ever flown a commercial flight or anyone who has ever wondered what it is like to be a flight attendant, but especially it is dedicated to my first four wing-sisters: Tracy Frame, Susan Evans, Sally "Blackie" Bartlett, and Melanie Feddersen. If you are interested in what happened to these former flight attendants after they left their careers, turn to the afterword, where I list what they are all doing today.

Contents

Introduction

As you read these stories you might ask, "Are these true? Did this really happen?"

The answer is yes—to most of the stories.

I really did get evicted from an apartment. I really did live in a tiny camper in the front yard of a friend of mine for a few weeks. I really did call up the airline and pitch myself to them in the third person, I really did work in a size 2 uniform once when I wore a size 12, and I actually have a photo of me in an overhead bin. And both the wig story and the toupee story really happened. But you should know right from the onset that I did change some details in certain stories in this book to protect both the innocent and the potentially embarrassed.

CHAPTER 1

My First Flight

I f you can't be Miss America and you can't be a model, then you become a flight attendant." The flight attendant sitting next to me was explaining why she decided to go for this job.

She was a former Miss Southern Some-Kind-of-Fruit State, she said. And when she didn't get crowned Miss America, her daddy said, "You need to get away and grieve the loss." He thought travel would help. So he called up his good friend, the president of our airline, and said, "My little Peaches here needs a job." She went on and on with the details. "Since I wasn't ready to marry Mr. Frank Barnell Jeffreys III...quite yet, Daddy said this job was a good one for a girl who was pre-engaged. He said it would keep me busy so Mr. FBJ would not grow tired of me before the wedding."

I could understand that. I was growing tired of her, and we had only just met. I was also hoping she wouldn't ask me why I took this job.

"Why did you take this job, honey?" she said, leaning into me as she bit a piece of celery without it touching her lipstick. "I mean"—she pointed the celery at me—"with you being so old and all." (She was twenty-one. I was thirty.) "And…so big." She used her celery to draw a huge circle of air around me.

She was five foot two and wore a size 0. I was six feet tall and wore a size 10. My shoe size was double hers. I felt like a Siberian work dog being taunted by a toy poodle. But I was too intimidated to bark at her, so I decided to tell her the truth.

"I'm trying to get over a loss too," I said.

"Honey, what do you mean? Did you lose your husband?" She held the celery directly under my mouth and moved in closer, like it was a microphone and she was the media.

I grabbed the celery and started speaking into it. "Well yes, you could say that. My fiancé left me for a younger woman."

Then I told Peaches the story of my life in a few sentences: how after college, I wanted to be a writer but instead became a recruiter for the fast-food division of a dog food company. And how I couldn't find true love until age twenty-seven. Then

I got engaged, and a few months before my wedding, my fiancé left me for a twenty-two-year-old. But he wasn't right for me anyway, I realized, and not just because he wasn't tall enough for me.

I could see Peaches loved the drama of my life. After my speech, she grabbed the microphone and bit it. Then she gave me a warning. "It will be hard for you now, being over thirty. The chances of you ever meeting anyone…well, you know… anyone with teeth, are just, honey, not good!" She stood and walked out of the galley, holding her hand near her hair as if adjusting an invisible crown.

I was left alone to ponder my fate.

She was right and I knew it.

I was doomed.

There was no hope.

I had lost my job, lost my fiancé, and lost my apartment. Now look at me, a big old work dog in flight attendant clothing.

CHAPTER 2

The Eviction Description

Getting evicted from your apartment, for anyone who is not familiar with it, is quite embarrassing. One day you come home confident that the late-night talk shows are fighting over you. And as soon as their guest coordinators battle it out, you're in. I mean, after all, you are the number one free-lance writer in the nation for the Charles Schulz *Peanuts* line for Hallmark! Sure, your name isn't on the cards, but you couldn't be more honored if the people who represent Disney said your mouse drawings look like Mickey.

And that very day over lunch, Charles Schulz himself said,

"Marsha, you have a voice. You need to design characters to go with your voice."

You are so bolstered by what good could come from this encouragement that you tell everyone who will listen that "Charles Schulz said I have a voice." You even call your land-lord (collect) and relay this information.

"Good," your landlord says. "Did you use that voice to ask him for the rent money?"

"No," you smile at her innocence. "That would not be act-ing cool."

She huffs and says, "Acting cool doesn't pay the bills."

You tell her not to worry, that you are destined for "the lists." (You mean *The New York Times* Best Sellers lists.)

Then your landlord says something very encouraging. She says, "Oh, I believe that. And the sheriff does too."

You have no idea what she is talking about because you have never known anyone who was evicted. You are, in fact, encouraged that she is being so supportive and has obviously been speaking well of you to her friends in law enforcement.

After the phone call to the landlord, you drive to your grandmother's place and hide your car behind a fence. (Your tags are a couple of years past due, and you have no insurance.)

Then, although you are twenty-nine years old, you catch the (free) old folks' shuttle to your apartment. On the shuttle, you stand up as if you are the tour guide and point out monuments and malls along the way. You don't charge for the ride, but many of the riders do tip you as they leave the bus.

As you trudge up the hill to the apartment complex where you've lived for three years, you contemplate dedicating your first book to your landlord: *To Lilly, who kept understanding and waited months to get paid.*

You reach your front door and realize some confused person has posted an ugly sign on your door. It says basically, "By Order of the Sheriff, Get Out." You absolutely cannot believe it. You won't sue anyone over this mistake, but it is the type of thing that could be embarrassing if someone saw it.

Then, as you read the fine print on the notice, you see your name, and it is spelled correctly. Your stomach tightens. You rip the sign off the door and go inside your apartment where you read the whole warning. You have twenty-four hours. Your things will all be placed on the front lawn of the apartment complex in twenty-four hours.

For one last second of denial, you think of some story. You were in Europe accepting the French prize for literature. (In this case it would be for literature not yet released from the mind of the writer.) Or drinking tea with a distant relative of Mark Twain and the tea went long. The bills must have arrived while you were out.

But then, numbingly, you realize this is no time for jokes. And somehow, in the next twenty-four hours, you must deal with your problem, which seems big. You have no family, no money, and no place to live.

You frantically gather all your belongings, except clothes, and move them into a storage unit you know you can't afford. You load your clothes in the backseat of your car. There are three cans of tomato soup rolling around in your trunk. (You would have put your clothes in the trunk, but it's raining and the trunk leaks badly.)

You drive to the front yard of the brother of your best friend, and as you get out of your car, your best friend gets out of her car too and tries to cheer you up.

"Well, look at that," she says.

You are looking. And like someone who has just been in a collision with life, you are in shock.

"I can't live in this!" you say, staring at a tin can disguised as a camper.

CHAPTER 3

The Beverly Hillbillies Without the Beverly

W ell, at least you don't have to worry about a roommate," said Janie, looking on the bright side. We stared at the camper before moving me in.

Janie had been my closest confidante for ten years, and as we stood side by side at what seemed more like a collision than a crossroad in my life, I glanced at her and thought about how she already had everything I wanted. She was married to the love of her life, had a beautiful baby, and was even the same kind of writer I dreamed of being—the kind that was supported by someone else.

She understood I was too stressed to accept her offer of moving into her tiny home with her family. Or of moving in with her brother's family, in front of whose home the camper sat.

"I'd rather live alone in my cardboard box," I said. Of course, I didn't mean it. I wanted to live alone, but not in a cardboard box. I wanted to live alone in my lovely apartment where I had lived for a long time. I wanted class, beauty, and a pool. I didn't want to be homeless.

"I can't believe I'm homeless!" (I had to yell to be heard over the sound of cars driving up and down the street.)

"Oh, come on," Janie yelled back, "you're not homeless. You're living in a camper...with a lawn and everything."

"I'm on the street," I screamed, but the traffic had stopped at that moment. The scream sounded like some kind of call for help—which maybe it was.

"No!" said Janie. "You're a full six inches off the street. Look, measure from the street to the first step to the camper. That's almost six inches. You can't say you're on the street."

"This camper has no electricity. And no running water." I moaned.

"Not true," said Janie. "What do you call this?" She pointed to the naked bulb stuck in the front window powered by an orange extension cord. The cord, fifty-five feet in length, stretched from the camper window to a bedroom window in the small bungalow that housed Janie's brother, his wife, their two boys, a three-legged dog, a psychotic cat, fish that were carnivores, and a hamster sitting in a wheelchair on the front porch. I preferred privacy to chaos.

"But no running water," I said.

"Look," said Janie. "You can just step out on the front step here and pour this bottled water over your hands, giving you running water. And it's a short walk to use the toilet in their home. They've provided you with an umbrella for when it rains."

I must have looked morose. "Janie," I said, "I feel like someone from the Beverly Hillbillies without the Beverly."

"No, you've got the Beverly. Look at you! How many homeless people are dressed in designer suits?"

It was true. I still had my wardrobe from when I had money and a secretary and a company expense account. The next day, I took the free shuttle to get my car and started applying for jobs. Any job. Every job. But I was turned down for being overqualified for low-paying jobs and undereducated for high-paying jobs. The fact that I had attended college for five years and never graduated was an obstacle to getting any other great job like the one I had left months before.

I had been hired for that job after I pitched my positive

points on the phone and showed up for the interview without ever sending in my résumé. I'd worked there a year and a half, making great money and feeling confident that working nine to five was only a temporary thing. My fiancé, Jeff, was going to rescue me (via marriage) from the corporate world. Then I would stay at home with a cup of tea and my typewriter and become America's answer to Tolstoy—but with more humor.

When Jeff left me for a younger (and more toned) woman, I lost it. In what can only be described as a moment of mental flatulence, I quit my day job and hibernated to begin writing. I don't think I had given quite enough consideration to the one benefit of being employed that I'd miss most: paychecks. It turns out they stop paying you after you quit.

"Not to fear," I told everyone. "I'm focused here. I'll just stay home and write. I have enough savings for six months!" (How long could it take to win a Pulitzer anyway?)

I ran out of money in three months, and you know the rest.

My getting evicted from the apartment caused me to re-think everything I had previously considered. For example, that dedication to Lily the Landlord was out.

We used to have a saying in personnel: "It's easier to get a job when you have a job." Meaning, when other companies want you, you're more marketable. Out of a job, you reek un-employment. Personnel managers are repelled by the smallest whiff of that.

At least I didn't *appear* homeless when I applied for work. I had an actual physical address. I simply used the home address of the people who owned the yard where the camper sat. My mail would come to the home of Janie's brother. In an effort to cheer me up, they would send the mail to my camper by tucking it under the collar of the dog and having him walk to the camper and scrape the door. Once they wheeled the mail over with the hamster sitting on it.

My third week in the camper was my point of deepest despair. The résumé thing was still holding me back. I'd make it to the third round of interviews for a job, and then someone would look at my résumé and realize I had no actual degree.

I needed a job that hired on first impressions. And I needed to make a first impression that would override any need to view my résumé.

Finally, sensing I was on the edge of running away to a warmer climate where living on the street would be easier, Janie took me out to eat and tried a psychological exercise she had just learned.

"Marsha, let's pretend. Let's say you could choose any job you want. Not the ones you've been applying for, but any job. Any job in the world. Describe to me what that job would be like."

"Travel and lots of it," I said immediately. I love pretending.

Janie was writing down everything I said, so I continued, "And I wouldn't have to pay for the tickets or the hotel or the food." I was on a roll. "And I'd have no responsibilities once I got to the destination. I mean, this would not be traveling to corporate meetings. I'd be on my own to be a tourist when I got to the destinations."

"Where do you want to travel?" said Janie.

"Everywhere. London, Madrid, Rome, New York, San Diego."

"And," Janie prompted, "what else? Come on, we're dreaming here."

"I wouldn't be forced to do any paper-type work: no reports to write, no résumés to review, just a job I would never take home with me, like being a waitress—only for more money. And it needs to have some glamour. And I don't want to work more than fifteen days a month and still make enough to live on.

"I'd have tons of time off to write the great American novel. And I'd get to meet lots of interesting people, and I'd never have to work with the same people over and over, and—"

Janie interrupted me. "It's what I thought," she said. "You need to be a flight attendant. It's the only job for you."

"But I have no idea how to get hired for that job!" I said. And I didn't.

"Pray about it," said Janie, and then she quoted what has to be the most famous verse in the history of war and peace. " 'The Lord is my shepherd...' Shep herd. Let him herd you."

"I'm not a shep," I said. "He herds shep."

"Sheep, he herds sheep."

"Shep is the singular of sheep...in my mind, anyway."

"We are 'the sheep of his pasture.' Try it," said Janie. "Ask for herding in the right direction."

So I did. And nobody believes this part, but it's true. A few days later, I was up at three on a Wednesday morning sitting in the depressing camper with the naked light bulb burning through the dark around me, and I saw an ad for the job of my dreams. It read: "Tour the world. Fly around in style. Be an international flight attendant. Applications accepted on Monday and Tuesday only. *No one* considered after that day."

It was a Sunday paper; I was reading it on Wednesday. I was a day late and a dollar short, as my grandfather used to say. (But this was the same grandfather who told me to learn Morse code so I'd never be out of a job.)

I studied the ad and realized that all I had to do was find a way to make showing up a day late for the interview of my life...an advantage instead of a disadvantage.

There were still several hours until the place opened for business and I could call them, so I decided to drink a little tea and then take a nap. I adjusted my light bulb and used a candle to boil a cup of water to make tea, which I drank with a lot of sugar. I went back to sleep until about nine, when it would be safe to call about the job.

CHAPTER 4

Getting the Job
of My Dreams

At exactly 9:00 a.m., I let myself into the house, avoiding the cat sitting on the stove, the three-legged dog on the couch looking out the window at the hamster, and the meat-eating fish. I got the phone, which had a very long cord, and pulled it out to the camper. I needed privacy as I dialed (literally) for dollars.

I prayed God would herd me to deliver the pitch of my life. Then I comforted myself with the fact that I had nothing to lose, except the job of my dreams, which it seemed I'd already lost. I mean, I was a day late for the interview.

Reading the ad again before I dialed, I realized the number provided at the bottom was for an outside recruiting firm—a recruiting firm I had actually used when I was a big shot in personnel. This would make it easy; I'd appear as one of them. Or better yet, as someone who used to employ them.

Wise as a serpent and gentle as a dove. Those words kept going through my mind as I started speaking to the girl who answered the phone. "Hi, I'm Marsha Marks." (Except that I used my maiden name and acted like they should recognize it.) Fortunately, they did.

"Hi, Marsha, we haven't heard from you in so long. How are you?"

"I am just great. But listen, I only have a minute, and I need to get some information from you. You know that ad you guys ran in Sunday's paper about the airline?"

"We're done with that." The girl was matter of fact.

"Yeah, I know." I tried to sound casual. "I was just wondering what airline that ad was for. I mean, I know you're done, but my friend and I are just curious."

"World Tour Airlines," she said. "Okay," I said. "That's cool. They're here in the Bay Area, right?" (It was a guess.)

"San Francisco," she said.

"Right."

As soon as I hung up the phone, I called information and got the number. Then I called World Tour Airlines and asked to speak to the person who hired the firm that placed the ad. I knew that if I asked to speak to personnel, I'd never get through. Or worse, if I told them I wanted a job, I'd never get through. So I said I had a question about the ad. Which I did. My only chance to get through was by identifying myself as a former personnel manager with a question.

The recruiter for WTA came on. "Hi," I said. "I'm Marsha Marks, and I noticed the ad from last Sunday's paper."

"We're done with that," she said, ending her part of the conversation.

"Yes, I know, but I just wanted to tell you, as a former personnel manager for"—I inserted the name of the parent company I used to work for—"I've come across someone who would be perfect for that job. She didn't see the ad until today, and I just wanted to tell you that, quite frankly, you missed a fabulous person. I mean, I've worked as a personnel manager for a long time"—a year and a half was a long time in my book—"and this person is amazing."

I gave a low whistle as if looking at the person right that moment. "I can't tell you how perfect she would be for you. She is tall and gorgeous"—hey, some people would say that—"and thin"—if you count low double-digit sizes thin—"and outgoing, funny, and gregarious! I'm so sorry you missed her."

"Does she speak any foreign languages?" she asked. She

was at ease now that she could see I was a fellow recruiter, a kindred spirit in the field of personnel.

Now, I could say hello in about eight different languages. So I answered honestly. "I don't think she's, you know, fluent in any other language. *But* she can say hello and things in at least eight languages. I'm telling you, I wish I could hire her. She is so amazing. She could be a model. She just lights up a room when she walks in."

I was on a roll now.

"Wow! She sounds wonderful. I mean, if she's half what you're saying, she sounds great. Who is she?"

I took a deep breath. Sometimes, all that's needed in a pitch is a dramatic pause. "You're speaking to her," I said.

The roar of laughter at the other end of the line told me I had her. "You're kidding? You're kidding me?" She kept saying that. Then, I heard her call someone over and repeat the whole pitch. Finally she said, "Hold on a minute."

When she came back on the line, she said, "You missed the first cut, but we're doing our second and third interview cuts tomorrow. Can you be in downtown Oakland at eleven?"

"Yes," I said. I had to act like this was a better deal for them than for me. "I'll be there!"

"Now, you don't have the job," she said. "You still have to make the second, third, and fourth cuts. But you just talked yourself past the first interview."

And past a résumé screening, I thought.

I showed up, made the cuts, and that's how I got my first flight attendant job a day late for the interview.

After training, the company paid to move us to different bases, so I was able to leave my tin can in the front yard. Not a moment too soon either. The owner wanted her camper back. She said she wanted to sell it as an antique.

CHAPTER 5

The Benign Tumors

There was another reason why the flight attendant job was perfect for me. I had not discussed this reason with Janie. Of course, she knew about it but had never brought it up after she heard the diagnosis. I think she was trying to spare me more emotional trauma.

I had been diagnosed with benign tumors.

I know you're thinking, *Benign tumors? If they are benign, where is the emotional trauma in that?*

Well, I didn't know they were benign when I discovered them, okay? I thought they were something horrible. I knew they were disfiguring and fast growing. I mean, I had observed them. And I had already spent a lot of time mourning the loss of my legs, my mobility, and my life potentially cut short. Which, quite frankly, had worn me out. Mourning takes a lot of energy, even when you're simply mourning what might happen.

I first noticed the tumors growing at the tops of my legs about six months into the personnel manager job. My first six months on that job were a whirlwind of furnishing my new office, attending lavish celebration dinners and big business lunches, and working long hours trapped behind my desk. And on weekends, I had to go into the office to catch up on endless paperwork.

I'd bought a lot of suits for this corporate job and was chagrined to realize that just when I thought I had gotten a job where I could wear anything I wanted, I couldn't. Uniforms were as much the order of the day in corporate America as they were on waitress jobs. It's just that the uniform was a dark fitted suit with a soft tailored blouse. It was a lot more expensive than a waitress uniform, and my company didn't pay for it.

It was because of those uniforms that I first noticed the tumors. There was one particular suit that suddenly looked funny around my thighs. On closer inspection, I noticed the growths. Abnormal, irregular growths. Precancerous, or perhaps horribly rotting, full-of-something-worse-than-cancer growths.

I called an oncologist and described them. Irregular in appearance, about six inches in length and two inches wide. Yes, they definitely had been growing at a very fast rate. In fact, they weren't there just six months before. The nurse was alarmed and rushed me right in. I felt sorry for the person who had to be canceled to make room for me, but she was just a surgery follow-up. I was, quite possibly, near death.

The doctor had a thick German accent, but his nurse spoke perfect English. She was there while he examined my tumors and spoke softly to calm me down. The doctor looked at the tumors and listened as I told him when they first appeared and how fast they were growing. He poked them and moved them slightly. He studied them for what seemed like several minutes. The office was deathly quiet while he and I looked at my legs and I began to realize how much I'd miss them.

Tears filled my eyes at the thought of what would be.

I'd already called everyone I knew who prayed, including the head of the prayer committee at a large church in my town. I could hardly speak by the time I got her on the phone, I was so caught up in the emotion of my tumors.

Weeping, I told her how I discovered them and that I'd been so busy on my job, I just hadn't noticed them before, but now the day was here for the appointment with reality. I'd heard she had a prayer chain that would alert five hundred people by phone. They would call each other, one by one, and each one would pray that I'd be brave enough to face the fate I had to face.

The doctor looked up from his examination. He sat back in his chair and pushed his glasses up to the top of his head. He spoke, but his accent was so thick I could hardly understand him.

"Vat vee have here is cellulite."

I had never heard of cellulite. I thought it might be a new type of tumor.

"Cellulite?" I said, crying openly now. "What kind of tumor is that?"

"Vat kind of tumor? Zees a Food Activated Tumor," he said. "Ze acronym is F-A-T."

Oh my, it was worse than I thought. I had activated tumors. And who would ever believe it, horror of horrors, tumors that were activated by food? Then slowly, like sunrise over the ocean, it began to dawn on me. Food Activated Tumor. Initials are F-A-T.

"F? A? T? Are you saying I'm fat? A food activated tumor?" I was incredulous. "You're saying I'm fat, aren't you? Well, I can tell you right now, I'm not fat. I never have been fat. And I never will be. It's impossible. I mean, they called me Olive Oyl in grade school because I looked like Popeye's girlfriend. I am not fat."

The oncologist suddenly felt sorry for me. He started asking me questions about my job. He helped me to realize the tumors had not been there before the desk job. And that I had been eating a lot of rich food and sitting at a desk for ten hours a day.

"Not exercising at all," he said. "You're not young anymore. Your metabolism has slowed down." (I was barely twenty-nine years old.)

I left his office. And realized I had to get a job that involved a little exercise.

But first I had to call that lady who headed up the prayer chain. She said she would be waiting for my update.

"How did it go?" She said gently. "Have they scheduled surgery?"

I didn't want to tell her about the whole awful discovery of Dr. Shocking Truth. So, I just said, "They are using another means to shrink them because, actually, they are benign. Benign tumors."

This experience was the beginning of my wanting to get out of corporate America. Out of a job where all I did was sit and eat and then go out and eat. I needed a job offering a little more exercise.

Although the job of flight attendant hadn't come up yet, I would remember the tumors when it did and think, *Now this is a job where you can move around all day, not sit watching tumors.*

Throughout my first twenty-two years of flying, I never told another flight attendant about my tumors. They disappeared about six months into the job anyway. We really did walk around a lot.

CHAPTER 6

Training

The year I started training, nobody hired older flight attendants like me (thirty years old). Most of the trainees were twenty-two or twenty-three years old. (Later, hiring women over forty became the vogue, and sometimes we hired people who had already retired from other jobs.)

I survived flight attendant training by telling myself I could do anything a twenty-two-year-old could do. I was wrong. It turns out that the twenty-two-year-olds were better at going without sleep and appearing coherent. I had a double problem with the no-sleep issue. First, I'd get so excited I couldn't sleep. Second, I couldn't function when I didn't get any sleep. The night before my first international flight, I stayed up all night, packing and repacking. We were allowed one suitcase and one personal bag. The whole day before the first flight, I cleaned my apartment as if I'd never come back.

This would become a habit over the years before each of hundreds of trips. Cleaning—when I had no time for it—would become suddenly urgent. (Someday, in therapy I'll figure out why.) I didn't even take a nap before reporting. (I was too excited.)

So I showed up for my first international trip having already been awake for twenty-four hours. Then I worked a twelve-hour flight to Rome, and in those days we had no breaks, not even a comfortable seat to sit in for a minute. Nearing the end of that first flight, when I had been awake for thirty-six hours, the supervisor came up to ask me my "check flight" questions. Check flight questions come on the first flight, after six weeks of classroom training, and they are the last phase in passing the flight attendant course.

She looked at me. At least, I think she was looking at me—exhaustion made her appear in triplicate. She asked me how to open the galley door. I smiled and told her I didn't remember. Then she asked me where the life rafts were located. I told her I thought they were in the ceiling. Then she asked why I was leaning to one side. I told her I was so tired I thought I was going to vomit and didn't want to shower her.

Every other flight attendant on the plane thought I was going to be fired. And I did too, but I was comforted by the fact that at least I'd get to sleep first. My first twenty-four hours in Rome, I saw the walls of my hotel room and ordered room service once so I did actually see the hallway, but nothing else. On the flight home I was so rested that my retake of the check flight went great. I appeared coherent and lucid, and I knew all the answers. Passed with flying colors, as they say.

During the entire flight home, I was exceedingly frustrated about not being able to sightsee on my first trip outside America. And exceedingly excited about the fact that this was the coolest job in the whole world.

I remember thinking after just one flight, *I would pay them to let me do this job.*

CHAPTER 7

A Whole Lot of Glamour

O nce I got out of training, I began to appreciate the glamorous aspect of my job. I remember walking with twelve other flight attendants through San Francisco International Airport. We were all in matching uniforms: dark two-piece suits. All of us wore the same amount of makeup, and we were tall and slender (the weight restrictions were strict). We were all perfectly groomed with straight teeth and the same hairdos, sprayed into perfect puffs. We walked in step and carried the same matching accessories. Crowds parted. Crowds stared. It was fun. I felt like something other than a poor, formerly homeless wannabe writer.

Soon after getting out of training, I realized another benefit of being a flight attendant. It had to do with my secret desire to be the life of the party—or a stand-up comedian. I could be funny on the plane and the people loved me. So I developed a little comedy routine. I'd use the same jokes over and over, and people would laugh their heads off. My jokes were simple. Like when we were in minor turbulence, I'd pick some slender guy and say, "Sir, you're going to have to sit still, you're rocking the entire aircraft."

Or I'd be picking up trash in the aisle of the aircraft and say, "Trash? Trash?" And then, I'd look right at someone and say, "It's not a personal comment. Trash?"

People laughed so hard at my jokes, I thought I was ready for Vegas. It was years later, when I tried actual stand-up at The Comedy Club in Los Angeles, that I realized I wasn't quite as funny as I thought. It turns out, if you take 180 people and strap them into a seat for eight hours, they'll laugh at anything.

CHAPTER 8

The Omniscient
Flight Attendant

Almost every day of my job, as I stand outside the aircraft boarding a flight, a passenger will run up and say to me, "Did my mother get on?"

I don't know this person's mother. I don't know this person. I assume the mother is a woman. And occasionally, I'm correct in assuming she might be older than the passenger. But to determine who this particular mother might be, I have to ask questions. "What is her name? What does she look like? Is she booked on this flight?"

I have a wing-sister who is a jokester. Whenever she gets asked that question, she pulls out two old photos she keeps in her pocket. She holds them up and says, "Which one is she, sir?"

CHAPTER 9

The Most
Embarrassing Thing

Several flight attendants and I were sitting in the back of the plane waiting for a mechanic to come fix whatever was holding our aircraft on the ground. We began talking about the most embarrassing thing that had happened to us during a trip.

My friend Paula won the prize. This is Paula's story, as she told it.

"It was the first flight of my career. You know how nervous you are on your first flight. We were doing Mexico City roundtrips"—we call them turns—"out of Los Angeles. We were on our way back and my stomach was killing me. I just didn't feel well. It was probably nerves."

"I was serving dinner on a 727 where the passengers sit three-across. When I reached over to serve the ten-year-old boy sitting by the window, he said something to me in Spanish. He was speaking so softly I didn't hear him, so I leaned in close to him and asked him to repeat what he had just said. He looked at me—and then he threw up. All over my head, shoulders, and my hand, because in those days we wore scoop-necked uniforms, and I was holding the top of my uniform as I leaned over the people in C and D seats.

"I was stunned. For a few seconds, I just looked at the kid with whatever had been in his stomach dripping off me.

"Then—and I have to tell you I'm mortified I did this, but the sound of vomit gets to me, and the smell, and I wasn't feeling well, anyway—I just...well, threw up back on him."

At this point, we all screamed, "*No!* That didn't happen!"

"It did," she said. "It was so embarrassing, and being my first flight and all, I thought I was going to get fired."

Paula went on to tell us that she cleaned up the mess as best she could and changed clothes. She helped the little boy

CHAPTER 10

The Former President of the United States, the Secret Service, and Me

M y fellow flight attendants and I soon became pretty relaxed on the airplane. So relaxed that we sometimes played jokes on passengers we knew. One was the overhead bin joke, where we'd climb into an overhead bin before people boarded and then jump out at unsuspecting passengers as they opened the bin to store their luggage. We played this joke on new-hire flight attendants and pilots stowing luggage for their first-check ride.

One day I had just climbed into the overhead bin at 37C because the brother of my fellow flight attendant would be traveling with us, and she wanted to "surprise" him. The door hadn't been snapped shut for more than one minute when I heard tapping and a stage whisper, "Marsha, get out of the bin! Get out of the bin now!"

Then the bin door opened and I yelled, "Gotcha!" No one moved. I was facing three Secret Service men—not the flight attendant's brother—who were now talking furiously into their wrists.

"We've got her. Roger. Yes, we see her now. Extra flight attendant found in 37C. No, not *at 37C. In bin 37C.* Exiting bin now. Correct. Flight attendant is climbing down from bin. Roger. Over and out."

Hey, how could I know that former president Gerald Ford was traveling First Class on our flight that day? Or that his Secret Service agents would do a preflight security sweep, which included accounting for every flight attendant?

I was asked to produce ID and an explanation as to why I appeared to be stowed away in the overhead bin. I wanted to make a joke and say, "Hey, you're not the only one checking for bugs," but no one appeared to be in the right mood.

At any rate, it was a long time before we ever played the overhead bin joke again.

CHAPTER 11

Speaking Southern

When the airline I worked for on the West Coast merged with an airline in Atlanta, those of us who weren't familiar with a Southern accent found ourselves in new territory.

For example, I was on the first flight where my California coworkers came into contact with a genuine Southern belle, complete with a thick Georgia accent. During the flight, we had to ask her to repeat almost everything she said so we could understand her.

When we landed in Atlanta, she stood up with us to say good-bye to all the passengers.

As the passengers deplaned, the Southern belle kept saying the same sentence over and over: "We're all in Georgia now. We're all in Georgia now."

Finally, the Californian lead flight attendant said to her, "I think they know they are in Georgia."

"What?" said the Southern belle, making the word "what" into three syllables.

"I think they know we are in Georgia now. You keep saying, 'We're all in Georgia,' and I think they know that."

The flight attendant from the South looked hurt as she explained, "I'm saying, 'We all enjoyed ya, now!'"

"Oh," said my West Coast coworker. "Oh. Well, that's okay then."

Another friend, Laurie, tells a story from her initial days working for an airline based in the Deep South.

"It was back in the seventies, and I had to go from a small town an hour north of Seattle, Washington, to Raleigh, North Carolina, for training. I was twenty-one years old, born and raised in the Pacific Northwest, and had never traveled east of I-5, nor had I ever met anyone who was from the Deep South.

"The first thing I remember about flight attendant training was how everyone was so into the way they looked and the designer clothes they wore or wanted to wear. Here I was in my grunge—before grunge became popular—and I definitely did not fit in.

"As we got settled into our dorms, I saw that I was the only trainee with just one bag and three pairs of shoes. Some girls had literally a different outfit for every day of the six weeks of training. I was further intimidated on the first day of class, before the teacher came into the room, when one Southern belle tugged on the sleeve of my dress and asked me if it was European.

"I had no idea if JCPenney was European, so I said, 'I don't know.'

"She tugged harder and, after looking around the classroom, asked again, as if I should know these things, 'Is that European?'

" 'I don't know,' I said, really loud this time.

" 'Well, kin I borrow it?' Even though she said this with a thick accent, it was clear what she was saying.

And I said a firm, 'No.'

"I didn't find out until lunch that she had been asking, 'Is that your pen?' She wanted to borrow the extra pen on my desk. The tugging on my dress was just a way to get my attention. 'Your pen' in Southern sounded just like 'European.' "

One more Southern speak experience occurred when we flew to Mobile, Alabama. It seems Mobile, Alabama, is one place where the residents feel compelled to let you know that the town name is pronounced not as it is spelled but as Moe Beal.

I saw an example of this fervor for pronunciation when we landed following a long flight. A passenger in the back of the aircraft stood up and rubbed his aching back. As he exited his row and grabbed his belongings, he said, "It feels so good to be mobile at last." Suddenly every passenger within ten feet turned to him and spoke in one voice: "It's *Moe Beal*."

So the next time you land in Mobile, Alabama—whatever you do—do not suggest anything about being mobile.

CHAPTER 12

The Offended Passenger

The airport in Fresno, California, is a small airport where stairs are pushed to the boarding door and passengers must climb up the steep stairs to enter our aircraft.

One day as I stood at the plane's boarding door watching our first passengers walk across the tarmac, I noticed that one woman, the first person coming toward our plane, appeared to be furious. She was an ample woman, and her entire body shook as she took each step, as if she were attacking the tarmac. She stomped up the stairs, appeared before me, and said, "I want to see the captain now! *Now!*"

"Can I help you?" I said, hoping I could at least diffuse a situation that must have occurred inside the terminal. "Is something wrong?"

"*Yes,* and I only want to discuss it with *the captain!*"

When the captain heard the ruckus, he stopped his pre-flight and came out of the cockpit. The angry passenger wasted no time. "I'd like to report that gate agent," she stated, pointing to the terminal. "He was extremely rude. The rudest man I've ever met!"

"What did he do?" asked the captain, grabbing a pen and paper to take notes.

The passenger held up her ticket jacket and exclaimed, "Look at what he wrote on my ticket!"

Sure enough, there in big, bold letters, in indelible ink, the agent had written the word *FAT* across the face of her ticket jacket.

"I am so sorry," I said. "It stands for Fresno Air Terminal." I grabbed the ticket from the passenger behind her. "See? He wrote it on everyone's ticket."

"Oh," said the woman, as she glanced at the other tickets with the word *FAT* across them. "Oh."

Then she turned and walked to her seat and never mentioned the incident again.

CHAPTER 13

What Do You Have in This Bag?

Every day passengers bring bags on board that they are not able to lift into the overhead bins. So they turn to me, and say, "Will you lift this for me? I don't want to hurt my back." I am tempted to say, "Oh, I *do* want to hurt my back! Here, let me."

Sometimes I think, *I can't lift fifty pounds over my head any better than you can.* Other times I simply ask a male passenger to assist me. Most times, though, especially if the person asking is a little old lady, I feel sorry for her and offer to carry her bags. That is how I got myself into carrying the heaviest bag I have ever lifted.

It was a shoulder bag. A woman who told me she was seventy years old came to the airplane in a wheelchair with her bag hooked on the back of the chair. I met her at the door and helped her to her seat. Then I went back for her bag. When I tried to lift it, I realized it must weigh close to a hundred pounds—more than twice our luggage limit.

I work out with weights. Even so, I was barely able to carry her bag to her seat and get it stowed. After the flight, she wanted me to carry the bag off the plane. I knew I couldn't ask anyone to help me, so I just went for it, huffing all the way up to the exit door.

"What do you have in here?" I could barely speak for the strain of carrying her bag. "Gold bullion?"

"No," she said sweetly. "Rocks. Lots of rocks. My daughter's house is next to a rock quarry. I just went over there and filled my bag with some big ones. For my garden and all, you know."

I set the bag down. And made a mental note: *Ask passenger if she has rocks in bag before offering to lift.*

CHAPTER 14

The Mistaken Beverage

We were doing trips from Seattle, Washington, to Juneau, Alaska. Juneau is a rugged place. And sometimes people who live in Juneau are there to get away from other people—especially those of us who live in the Lower 48.

It was not unusual for us to have "back-country residents" among our passengers on these flights from Juneau to Seattle. One day we boarded a guy who looked like he hadn't been out of the back country in years. In fact he told us that this was his first trip in thirty years to the Lower 48. He had to go settle a financial dispute in his family.

Not only had the man been away from the Lower 48 for thirty years, he also appeared to have been away from all showers, combs, or toothbrushes. But our job is not to judge, just to serve. So as soon as everyone was seated, the other flight attendant, whom I'll call Gini, and I prepared to serve lunch. We noticed Back-Country Juneau Man was sitting right across from our galley. We also noticed he was loudly hawking "loogies." A loogie, for anyone who isn't familiar with the term, is excess mucus that people cough up from deep within their lungs. They hack and cough and then spit. This man was using his beverage cup as his loogie container.

Gini (who was the sweetest flight attendant I've ever flown with) was the galley person setting up the trays. She had the oven doors open and alternated between kneeling to the bins below the ovens to get out set-up trays and standing to complete the trays with hot entrées. Then I would pick up the trays and run them out to the passengers. This was in the days of not only hot meals but a choice of entrée. We actually asked Coach passengers if they wanted "chicken or beef."

We were busy, so it's understandable that neither of us saw Back-Country Juneau Man get up from his seat and set his loogie beverage cup right next to Gini's cup on the back counter of the galley.

Gini was too busy to look behind her as she reached for her beverage. She took a big swig and realized something was very wrong. She looked down at the cup in her hand and realized she was not holding her own beverage. Just then Back-Country Juneau Man walked up looking for what he had left on the counter.

The service was detained for a moment while Gini ran into the bathroom and tried to vomit. She wasn't successful and asked me if I had any antiseptic mouthwash. I didn't.

We monitored Gini's health for weeks after that, but she never got sick. Some flight attendants even suggested the loogie drink was a sort of vaccine. Gini was not amused.

After that experience, we never let our beverage cups out of our sight.

CHAPTER 15

Marry Me, Fly Free—
on a Seat-Available Basis

The night I met my husband, I was one step away from buying a T-shirt that read, "Marry Me—Fly Free."

I thought we flight attendants needed to advertise this benefit of our job. I wanted to wear that shirt to a big party with sixty or so flight attendants and then invite a bunch of single guys. We'd meet and mingle, and maybe Mr. Right would be there. In an odd twist of fate, that is sort of how I met my husband. Except I wasn't wearing the T-shirt, and I wasn't the one who arranged the party.

Just before I met Tom, my entire family had turned against me for trusting God to bring me Mr. Right. "You're wasting the best years of your life," my grandmother had said. "You can't trust God for things like this!"

But I'd read a verse that essentially said if I trusted in God with all my heart, he would direct my paths.

I told that to my grandmother, and she said, "He's directing you down the path of loneliness. Do you want that? You're going to end up a shriveled old woman with no one to love you. Do you want that?"

I didn't want that, but neither did I want to become a casualty in the epidemic of divorces in my family. "I just have this idea," I said to my grandmother, "that if I leave the choice to God, he will direct me to Mr. Right. It's called trusting in the Lord."

"It's called blind faith, and there's a reason they call it that," she told me. "It's for people who are too blind to see the way."

"Grandma, it's better to be lonely single than lonely married."

"Rubbish," she said. "Now get out there and get yourself a husband."

When I met Tom I had almost given up on waiting for God to bring me someone. I was thirty-three years old and felt 103.

I was working for my second airline, West Coast Airlines. (When I was a little girl growing up in the Pacific Northwest, we used to watch commercials that said, "West Coast Airlines, the Only Way to Fly." And now here I was working for that airline.)

My fellow flight attendant trainees (all ninety-nine of them) and I were in Los Angeles to begin six weeks of training. Each airline has a unique training for its flight attendants. On our first night in town, before we started the official training, three of us talked the hotel van driver into taking us to Ralph's grocery store in the Manhattan Beach Village Mall. We wanted to stock up on food so we could save our per diem and use it for more important things—like getting our nails done.

It was in the fresh fruit section that two of us noticed a good-looking guy across the aisle, staring at our friend Mary. He seemed to be lingering around us, listening to our conversation, and falling in love.

Finally he spoke to us. "You girls are in flight attendant training?" He said it with a reverence usually used to address a movie star or something.

"Yes, it's our first day. We're starting six weeks of training."

"That's cool."

"Yeah, there are one hundred of us staying at a hotel in town, near LAX."

"That's cool." He looked at Mary, and then he said to all

three of us. "Listen, you guys, I'm a sales rep to aerospace engineers who work at companies here in Los Angeles. Why don't we get a party going? I mean, I'll get all the guys together, and you can get all your flight attendant friends, and we can meet at the restaurant in this mall on Friday night."

This was still in the days when flight attendants were hired, in part, because of their looks. All the flight attendants were actually told that they had to be tall and thin, have no blemishes, and have straight teeth. So I guess this engineer–sales rep felt the airlines had already done the visual screening for him. Or maybe he had heard our motto: "Marry me, fly free."

His suggestion struck us as weird. We thought he was nuts or blowing smoke. But Mary liked him, so she gave him the number to our hotel.

The next Thursday night, the guy called our room and said, "I've got twenty-one guys for the party tomorrow. How many girls did you recruit?"

Mary and I had each picked up a different phone, and a third roommate was listening in. We all looked at each other and said, "Just us."

We weren't stupid. Three girls, twenty-one guys—we'd have our pick. Plus, if the guys turned out to be odd (engi-nerds instead of engineers), we wouldn't be responsible for telling any other trainees about some boring party.

The truth was, I didn't really want to go to that party, but

I was afraid of these L.A. types and went to keep my two girl-friends from getting involved with anyone who might be something worse than boring. Once I got there, I immediately started to hate the whole party.

In my old personnel job, we used to say that the decision to hire is made in the first four minutes. I felt the same way about looking for Husband Material. It wasn't that I could decide if he was the one for me in four minutes, but I could certainly decide if he was someone I wanted to get to know. And I had already eliminated everyone at this party, or at least everyone I'd met.

After thirty minutes, I wanted to leave. I went looking for my girlfriends to tell them I was outta there. I was almost out the door when I saw him.

Across a crowded room, he stood talking to two other guys. He was tall and so good-looking he took my breath away. He wore a sweater over a button-down shirt. Conservative dresser—I liked that. (I was actually repelled by flash. I was drawn to men who didn't need to impress me with their open shirts or gold chains.) This guy seemed to be a man of charac-ter. It just showed on his face. I don't mean, character as in a *character*. I mean—as I later told his parents—he had God and country written all over him. (Tom's parents later told me that Tom was a former Eagle Scout—as if being an Eagle Scout explained his good character.)

Tom and I were married eighteen months after we met. Soon we'll celebrate our eighteenth wedding anniversary. I can honestly say he has been the most-appreciated gift God has ever given me. I prayed for Mr. Right and waited years, trusting a God who kept me waiting—until he sent someone who was worth the wait.

I wasn't the only one in the relationship who got what was only dreamed to be possible. Tom said he could hardly believe he was dating a flight attendant, much less marrying one. And his parents were thrilled with the fact that their only son, who had moved from Lincoln, Nebraska, to Los Angeles, could now fly home anytime he wanted. "Marry me, fly free—on a seat-available basis" was a hit with the whole family of the man of my dreams.

CHAPTER 16

Flying Free

Tom and I decided to wait a couple of years to have children. We wanted to enjoy life together. And we did. We began using our free-flight benefit on our honeymoon. We flew First Class to Maui for a week, then on to Oahu, which was in the middle of a rainstorm. Then we flew to the Oregon coast, which was in the middle of a heat wave.

During the first three years of our marriage, we flew to Colorado to ski, to New Mexico for dinner, and to Lincoln, Nebraska, at least three times a year to visit Tom's family. We flew everywhere and anywhere we wanted. The airline I worked for wasn't doing well financially, so there were always seats available—and most of those seats were available in First Class. We lived a life of vacation luxury. I would call up friends in New York and tell them I was flying in for lunch. I would call up friends in Washington, D.C., and tell them I was flying in for a visit to the museums.

When Tom and I were too poor to afford a hotel room and we needed a little excitement in our lives, we would say, "Let's fly to Atlanta for dinner and a movie."

"Wow," said my friends. "You have a special place in Atlanta to go to dinner?"

"No, we eat on the plane. In First Class, it's a four-course dinner. Then they show a movie. We sleep on the flight home."

"So let me get this straight," our friends would say. "You're not flying to Atlanta to attend dinner and a movie. You're flying to Atlanta and having dinner and a movie on the plane?"

"Yeah. It's great."

We would often meet people in First Class who weren't in our class financially. "So, what do you do?" we would ask before finding out they owned a baseball team or a line of grocery stores.

"What do you do?" they'd respond. I'd always say, "I'm a writer, almost finished with the great American novel." Then I'd confess that I also worked for the airline.

Tom worked as an aerospace engineer for a company in

Long Beach, California, until a bigger company in Seattle recruited him. When Tom agreed to that new job, we moved to Seattle. Our free-flight benefit was an advantage during the nine months we spent trying to sell our condo in Los Angeles.

We flew back to Los Angeles to check on the condo advertising, walk on the beach, and try to recover from the shock of moving to a place where it rained every day. Eventually, we did sell that condo, and for the next ten years, I flew out of Seattle. That's where Tom and I decided to start a family.

We have a saying in our home: "Flying free is heavenly." And all our friends who received buddy passes every year say, "We agree."

After more than twenty years on this job, I haven't gotten over the fun of deciding at the last minute that I'd like to fly across the country, showing up at the airport, and doing just that—flying free.

CHAPTER 17

Becoming Pregnant Just Before Joining AARP

In my first book, *101 Amazing Things About God*, I wrote about how we had our first child at age forty-five. What I don't explain in that story is that I was the only one who was forty-five. My husband, Tom, was in high school. Or he looked like it.

Tom is exactly eight years and ten months younger than I am. Round that difference to nine years, multiply by good genes, and divide by a short haircut (which makes him look like a teenager), and you have the basis for the high-school quip.

You may think I am exaggerating—as writers are wont to do—about how young my husband looks. That's why I've come prepared with actual documentation of humiliations I've endured while married to someone who was in third grade when I started college. And further humiliations I endured as a result of getting pregnant just prior to joining AARP.

In 1995, I was forty-four. Tom looked twelve.

We had no children yet. Tom and I were both working: he as an aerospace engineer, and I was a flight attendant who had a few ideas for books. At the time I was so low in seniority that the only flights the airline allowed me to work were all-night trips from Seattle to Anchorage, Alaska, and back.

I would leave at seven in the evening and get home at eight in the morning, and then I would try to get some sleep before working the next night. However, I never did get sleep because we had a neighbor named Greeta who was ninety years old and suffering from dementia.

Greeta loved crows. Every morning she'd put into practice the feeding of the five thousand. Standing in front of waves of crows, green scarf flying in the wind, she'd throw bread and promise free healthcare to all. The crows loved it. The cawing was so loud that it drowned out the occasional test run of a 747 engine at the Boeing aircraft company close to our home.

I confess that the reason I know so many details about Greeta is that in my half-jet-lagged, half-dead state with no sleep, I'd lose perspective on what really mattered. I'd pull a chair up to the window where, looking between the slats of the plastic blinds, I'd watch and take notes. I knew that years down the road, this would be good fodder for a book, and my lost sleep would not be in vain.

Golden Greeta the Crow Feeda went on for hours. Then just as she'd give up and wave her hand at the crows and say, "You'll never vote for me anyway," it would be time to get ready for another all-nighter from Seattle to Anchorage.

Now there is something you should know about being a flight attendant: there is no humidity on the aircraft. The air is so dry that if you leave a piece of roast beef out for two hours, it becomes beef jerky. Unfortunately, the air has the same effect on skin.

So me and my beef-jerky face finally finished three all-nighters in a row, and my refreshed, young husband met me at the gate. Then we decided to go to shopping for some new clothes for him.

We picked a famous department store near the Seattle-Tacoma airport. I was sitting outside the men's room when Tom came out to model new jeans. He stood in front of me and said, "How do you like these?"

I shook my head. "I don't think so, honey."

"I like them!" he said with a confidence that told me he was buying them.

Tom then went back into the dressing room and the sales clerk came over to comment. "At that age," she said, "you can't tell them anything."

At that age, you can't tell them anything. Suddenly I got it. She was confirming my worst fear. Tom was thirty-five years old, and she thought I was his mother. I kept opening and closing my mouth and couldn't think of a thing to say. That's when Tom came out and said, "Let's go."

Then he wrapped his arm around me and gave me a big kiss. The sales clerk watched in horror as she slowly realized that we weren't mother and son. Or maybe she just thought I was evil. I don't know. The whole thing was so humiliating, I try not to think about it.

A year later, I was seven months pregnant and in the mall in Bellevue, Washington. There was a woman sitting next to me who apparently had never seen a pregnant grandmother-type. Sitting next to an Eagle Scout. Who had his arm around her.

She kept staring at me. But in that endorphin state that God gives those who are pregnant, I didn't see myself as she did. I saw myself as a fresh, first-time mom (who maybe had let her roots slip, but what did it matter?). I had gained fifty pounds in the first seven months and had gone from model thin to fat and happy. I didn't care how I looked! The only thing that mattered was my belly, and I wanted that belly to stick out and shine.

The woman finally spoke. "Are you pregnant?" She asked the question as if she was shocked. Really shocked.

"Yes." I said, smiling. Then I thought I'd let her off the hook in case she was wondering. "I'm an older first-time mom."

"I'll *say!* How old are you?"

I squinted my eyes at her, and rage filled me for a minute. "Well, my husband is thirty-six!" I said. "So I can't be that old!"

These are the types of humiliations I experience every day.

I just thought you should know there are some downsides to being a flight attendant. There's the beef-jerky face and the all-night flights with no rest in-between. And if these problems aren't bad enough, they will seem worse if you marry a man who looks like he needs a note from his principal to go out with you and then you have a baby just before joining AARP.

CHAPTER 18

The Dream
of Becoming a Spud

W hen I was hired for my first airline job, I didn't understand the importance of seniority. In the business of in-flight service, seniority is everything. Seniority (your date of hire relative to other flight attendants) determines your bidding preferences for trips, vacations, and number of days off. I had such low seniority in the beginning years at all three of the airlines I worked for that I was on Ready Reserve. Ready Reserve means that you are on call twenty-four hours a day for several days a month. When I started out I was on call twenty-four hours a day for twelve days a month.

In those days we didn't have cell phones, so I lived with a beeper. Later, as I got more seniority, I moved to Call-in Reserve, which meant I could make a call in the morning and another one in the afternoon to see if Scheduling had a trip planned for me. Finally, I got to the place where I could Hold-a-Line. Holding-a-Line meant that I knew a full two weeks before any given month which days I would be flying and what trips I would be flying. But every year for the first twenty years of my flight career, I dreamed of becoming a Spud.

The term *Spud* was first brought to my attention by a flight attendant who walked up and warned me to stay out of the flight attendant lounge between the hours of three and four each afternoon.

"Why?"

"Spud sign-in," she said.

"What?"

"Spud sign-in. It will make you sick when you see the schedules they fly." She referred to the flight attendants with forty or more years of seniority.

"Look at them," she said. "They all wear the shapeless gray uniforms with brown spots, and their middles stick out farther than any other part of them. And as they turn on their thin legs, the thing that comes to mind is spuds. They all look like spuds on a stick."

Then she pulled out a schedule of one of the Spuds. "Look," she said. "They work eight days a month, get six weeks vacation a year, and make sixty-thousand dollars a year. That's just two days a week, working for six months of the year, and the other six months they are using a week of vacation each month, bunching their trips together and getting paid for not working."

"I'm warning you," she said. "If you go into the lounge when they are signing in, you'll just get jealous."

But all of us held on to the dream that someday, maybe someday, we'd have schedules like Spuds. We all dreamed of becoming a Spud.

In 2004, the year in which I'm writing this book, there have been major cutbacks on all the airlines. No longer are there salaries like the Spuds once made, and none of our flight attendants get six weeks vacation anymore. The good old days are gone, and with them went our dreams of ever becoming a Spud.

CHAPTER 19

Saving Lives

Y ou know what I like about this job?" asked Peaches as she sat next to me on the jump seat. "You do not have to use that side of your brain that is best left for scientists and such."

"You mean the left side of your brain?" I said, looking over my glasses at her.

"Yes, I prefer to lean to the right. Left thinking is for people who do not have looks." She paused and looked right at me, as if to make her point, then continued. "For me, it's just not right. I prefer using the part of my brain that takes care of personality and not particulars."

Then Peaches leaned in as if to share a secret. "And," she said, "when I try to use that left part of my brain, I sometimes get mixed up. Did you hear what happened to me in training?"

"No."

"Can you keep a secret?"

"No."

"Well, I mean, will it go no further than your closest friends?" She obviously wanted to tell me.

"No further unless I write a book one day."

"Honey, you are never gonna write a book. Come on, you are a flight attendant. We are not known for typing."

"I'm taking notes," I said, "but I won't use your real name."

"Or the name of my future husband, Mr. Frank Barnell Jeffreys III. Now, that would be humiliating. How long have you known how to type?" she asked.

"Peaches, just tell me the story."

"Okay, I was really trying to concentrate in training. But this one day, I had this tiny chip in my nail and it was snagging things, so I had to take care of it during class. I was filing it while the teacher was going on and on about how to save a life or something. She was shouting like some Southern Pentecostal."

"It was the health and safety drills?" I asked.

"Yes." Peaches nodded her head. "And—"

I interrupted her. "The teacher was shouting symptoms of a passenger who needed assistance?"

"Yes, and you know I don't like shouting, and she kept yelling, 'You've got a middle-aged man lying in the aisle, unconscious but breathing. What are you gonna do?' Well, I was just going to let someone else answer that question. But no one did answer it. Then the teacher yelled again, 'You've got a middle-aged man lying in the aisle *unconscious but breathing!* What are you *gonna do?*'"

"Peaches," I said, "she was shouting because we are supposed to be able to shout back our response. Remember our motto: Maintain life until help arrives?"

"Yeah, well, I was waiting for someone else to answer. But the teacher sees me furiously filing my little nail, behind my book, and points right at me and yells at me. I mean, she yelled each word as if it were a sentence in itself: 'You! You-have-got-a-middle-aged-man-lying-in-the-aisle-unconscious-but-breathing! What-are-you-going-to-do?'"

Peaches looked up and patted her hair. "I got flustered. I mean, I had studied what to do for an unconscious man, but I didn't understand this new problem, so I asked her."

"You asked her?"

"I raised my hand and said, 'I just have one question.' The teacher said, *'What?'* And I said, 'What is butt-breathing?' I mean, I had heard of 'unconscious' but not 'unconscious butt-breathing.'"

"I've never heard of it either," I said.

"I know," Peaches said. "Can you imagine how embarrassing it was? I mean, it took me about an hour to even get the stupid joke. It wasn't something you use CPR on. It was, you know. He was just unconscious, *but* he was breathing."

"Sure," I said. "We had never covered unconscious breathing of that type. It's virtually unknown."

"That is my point exactly," she said. Then she stood, turned, and placed her hand on the side of the galley wall. Striking a pose like something out of *Vanity Fair,* she said, "Honey, I wish you well with your typing project."

Before I could respond, she was gone down the aisle returning to her fans.

CHAPTER 20

Packing

During my career as a flight attendant, I have never gotten the packing thing down pat. I am always packing and repacking, in a panic, before every trip. I always forget something and take too much of something. For example, I'll pack five different hair products and forget an extra pair of shoes. Or I'll have three pairs of casual jeans but have to wear my work sweater with them because I forgot a casual shirt.

In recent years, we have not been allowed to bring as much luggage as we want. Now we bring one rolling bag and one small personal bag. We have to pack our uniforms and our change of shoes—we have concourse shoes and in-flight shoes.

We pack our manual, which is huge—the size of a three-inch thick text book—and our demo equipment, which includes an oxygen mask and a demo seat belt. We need casual clothes for when we land, and entertainment for the hotel room, which for me, includes at least six books to read. For others it's a CD player and CDs. I also bring my laptop computer to write the great American novel. Sometimes, I'll bring a paper copy of a new manuscript. And I can't forget my passport...and my airline ID...and my parking pass, credit cards, and cell phone.

This year a family built a new home next door to ours, and unfortunately, its front door faces our driveway. Here is an example of what that family might see when I'm leaving on a trip: woman wearing flight attendant uniform—me—carries luggage to car, gets in car, starts it up, and puts it in reverse; slams on brakes, scurries back into house, and gets ID; runs back to car, starts it up again, and backs carefully out of driveway; slams on brakes, runs back into house, and grabs manual that was forgotten; drives down street, turns car around, and races back to house; slams on brakes, runs in, and retrieves cell phone; scurries back to car and dials cell phone to list self on later flight because now she is too late for scheduled flight.

A psychotic packer is what they would see, and they probably think—like anyone would—that after twenty years as a
flight attendant, I'd have this whole thing down to a science.
But I don't.

CHAPTER 21

Forgetting My Uniform

O ne thing about being a flight attendant that is crucial: uniforms. The company (at least my company) pays for our uniforms. The company even pays to have them cleaned. So, our employer expects us to adhere to the rule of not showing up for work without them.

Uniforms are to airlines what uniforms are to the military. The uniform is how people identify the brand and what branch of a large organization we work for. Hours of training are spent on the fact that we, as flight attendants, are on the front line of brand recognition. I mean, next to the paint schemes on our fleet of planes, our uniformed personnel are it. We don't show up for work without our uniforms. Except…I did.

May I just say something here in my favor? It was a short trip—an unusual trip. From Seattle to Los Angeles, and back, with the first leg of the trip a "deadhead." This means that all I had to do was ride as a passenger to Los Angeles. And on a deadhead we can wear street clothes. Then I had a three-hour sit in Los Angeles before working the flight back home.

I loved trips like this. Read a book on the flight down, get paid flight time, work a short flight home, and be done. Due to the fact that I was so excited about this trip—allowed to dress in street clothes on the way down and packing extra beach clothes in case we were delayed in L.A.—I was bound to forget something. I always forget *something*. It's just that this time it was my…uniform. Oops.

Now, not wanting to get fired or even to draw any attention to my gaffe, I looked for a way to cover up my mistake. The problem was that I didn't realize the mistake until a few minutes before I had to report to my flight back to Seattle.

I'd waited until the last possible minute to change.

"Oh dear God!" was my prayer when I discovered I had nothing to change into. My next prayer was "Yikes!" "Oh man!" was my last utterance before it occurred to me to run to the lost-and-found closet. Usually that closet contains things left in the flight attendant lounge, things nobody bothered to claim. Things like old shoes, tattered aprons, sweaters with rips in the arms. But fortunately for me that day, the closet included two uniforms. Actually, one uniform and one apron.

I grabbed the uniform dress and noticed right away that it was tall enough for my size 12 tall figure. Then I saw the size and was unbelievably thrilled to realize that the uniform was also a size 12. I couldn't believe it...except something seemed not quite right. As I stepped into the bottom half of the dress and couldn't get it over my hips, I checked the tag again. That's when I noticed there was no 1 beside the 2. It was a 2. A size 2 tall.

I don't know if there are any readers who wear a size 12 and have tried to fit into a size 2, I mean seriously fit, but it doesn't work. I was finally able to wiggle my behind into this dress, but only because it had a pleat in the front and another in the back, both of which were now completely stretched out, making the former A-line skirt into something straight and tight.

I had one minute left to dress before checking into my flight. I grabbed the edges of the dress and shoved my arms into the half-length sleeves, which now barely covered the corners of my shoulders. They appeared to be what my mother called cap sleeves.

When I tried to close the bodice, I couldn't even get it within six inches of closing. I grabbed the spare apron and a bag of safety pins. I always keep safety pins. I pinned that apron securely to the front of the dress, because being a flasher would be worse than forgetting my uniform.

There are some things you just make the best of, I thought, as I casually walked up to the gate. I tried to act as if nothing was wrong. The flight attendants on board were from the Seattle base, and they all knew me.

As I came to the front entrance, the lead flight attendant looked at me and said, with her eyes as big as I have ever seen them, "What…do you have on?"

I tried to tell her what happened, but she wouldn't listen to my explanation.

She picked up the intercom to alert all the other crew members.

"You guys have to get up here and look at what the cat drug in. You will never believe it!"

The laughter eventually died down. Weeks later. Not, unfortunately, during that entire flight. Every time my fellow crew members looked at me, they started laughing.

But one flight attendant had mercy on me and gave me her sweater to wear. "Button it up all the way," she said, "because a size 2 dress on a size 12 body—well, that ain't gonna fly."

I was never happier than when that flight was over. And I've never forgotten my uniform again.

Flight Delays

In all my years of flying, I have to confess at least a third of my flights are held up by some kind of delay. The average customer does not realize that on any given day many variables can affect the on-time departures and landings of the two thousand flights on my airline alone. Variables having to do with things like weather, mechanical issues, crew, luggage, and cargo.

No matter what the delay, once we do take off, passengers ask me the same question, and they ask it the same way: "Am I going to make my connection?"

I have never seen them before and don't know what their connections are, so I look at them and say, "No."

Wait, I *don't* say no. That would be rude. Instead I explain what I hope is the case—that we have notified the gate agent of our late arrival and that often, if one flight is delayed, their connecting flights are delayed also.

But the passengers do not see me as a mere mortal. I know this because after I answer them with all I know, they get angry and say, "Perhaps you don't understand!" And then they tell me in detail why they need to make their connection. "We are going to a wedding" or "We have a connecting flight to catch to our cruise."

The passengers assume that if I understand they are going to miss the first day of their cruise or their Uncle Jeff's wedding or something more important, I'll say, "Well, why didn't you tell me? In that case, I'll just rip the wings off and we'll become a rocket."

Or that I'll say, "Oh! You didn't tell me it was your *first* cruise. Rachel, call the captain! Tell him to run every red light!"

CHAPTER 23

The Day I Was Deemed
a Security Threat

I n early 2003 I arrived at the airport in full flight attendant uniform, ready for my flight. I had to go through the extensive security and waited in line with the other passengers. Then I was told to step aside, as I was randomly selected for further screening. This isn't too big a deal. When you travel for a living, it happens quite often. Usually, they wand your bag (running a little screening cloth over it), and you're back on your way.

This time, however, I didn't get my bag back. In fact, I watched as more and more security guards were called over. They all started talking nervously and repeating, "Extra tests." Then they began chattering in low tones, and several of them looked at me as if they now recognized me...from *America's Most Wanted*.

Then I noticed that police with guns that might be loaded were moving toward me.

But this was all a huge mistake. I was confident there was nothing actually wrong. I mean, come on, I'm a flight attendant who writes like Shakespeare—if Shakespeare were a flight attendant. And as for being patriotic, I couldn't be more patriotic. I loved God, country, and Dave Barry. I was sure my name would be cleared in moments.

Then suddenly, a huge, scary guy was spitting words at me. "Ma'am," he said with barely controlled anger, "we've got a problem here. Your bags test positive for bombs."

"You're nuts," I said. (May I just say here that I now know it's not a good idea to tell a spitting guard he is nuts.)

I saw the guard start shaking with fury.

"Retest the bag!" I said. I was disgusted. This was ridiculous.

"We've tested it six times."

Now more guards were looking down on me. (They hated me. They knew I was evil. They had the proof. And they weren't about to be charmed away from the facts—not that telling someone he's nuts is charming.)

Still, I wasn't that nervous. "You have to be joking," I said, wanting to elbow them to show I got the joke.

"We are not joking," said Sergeant Friday. "We are not joking at all, ma'am."

They wanted me to confess. They kept asking me questions about how positive indicators of copious amounts of explosive residue could appear on my bags. "Weapons residue, ma'am."

Every time they said "ma'am," I couldn't get over how it came out sounding like "scum."

"There is," they said, "even residue in the *contents* of your bag. Your bags are coated in it."

I had no explanation, but I stopped telling them they were nuts. After half an hour of their accusing me, I had begun to realize an actual arrest could be in the works. That thought drained my sense of humor.

It was so hard to believe this was happening. I mean, I watch the Crime Channel, but I never expected to be part of what was obviously a false accusation. Nobody seemed to believe there was no way this could all be true.

"I don't even own a firearm," I said. "And *no,* I don't really know anyone who actually carries one. And *yes,* my husband goes on pheasant hunts—but they don't use TNT to kill the birds!"

On and on they questioned me, and for the first time in my life, I understood the forced confession syndrome. I was almost willing to say anything they wanted to hear just to get out of there.

Other passengers going through security heard their questions and were now narrowing their eyes, as if to say, "Where there is smoke, there is fire," or in this case, "Where there is bomb residue, there is an evil flight attendant."

Thirty minutes into the interrogation, I asked for a phone and called one of the in-flight supervisors. She was new on the job and didn't know my clean record. She simply advised me to get myself a lawyer.

The thing was, I wanted a lawyer, but I was afraid if I asked for one they would assume my request was an admission of guilt. I was terrified by then—one hour into the interrogation—and I began to cry. Still they wouldn't let me go until *two hours* later, after they told me I was considered a threat to the aviation industry and had to leave the airport immediately. (I was only allowed to leave because no actual bombs were found—just residue.)

I was shaking when I got home, and when I went to bed that night, I couldn't sleep. Finally, in the wee hours of the morning, I called the twenty-four-hour security desk at my company and told the whole story. I was patched into some-one who handled problems like this, and with a quick look at my prior flight schedule, she solved the whole conundrum.

"Marsha, why didn't you tell them about your flight last month? You know, the one where you volunteered to work a military charter with two hundred armed soldiers and weapons and ammunition all over the cabin?"

"Oh yeah," I said. "That was when I was trying to bring peace and love to all mankind. To do my good deed for my country." (It seems, every time I try to do something good, it ends in a Lucille Ball–type episode; for example, volunteering to work a military charter and subsequently being declared a threat to aviation and banned from going within five hundred yards of any FAA facility.)

"If you had them call us," the security person said, "we would have explained you are a qualified, specially trained, military-charter flight attendant volunteer."

"I'll do that next time," I said.

Corporate security soon cleared things up. After recommending I use rubbing alcohol to clean my bags, the powers that be decided I could be allowed back into the airport.

And as I write this, I have almost completed the therapy necessary to cope with the day I was deemed a threat to America and especially the aviation industry.

Flight Attendant Flip-Out

We were working the Los Angeles to Las Vegas turns again, and this was before the days of the "fast break" (abbreviated) service. Passengers did not realize that thirty-seven minutes of flight time minus ten minutes for landing and another ten minutes to level off after takeoff left approximately seventeen minutes to serve 170 people.

Some passengers get very excited when they see the beverage cart in the aisle. Maybe it's their first flight and they want to take full advantage of the experience. Or maybe they just think, "Wow, a full beverage cart. I wonder what's on it."

On this flight, I was working with my friend Kay. We were rushing to get through the entire cabin in seventeen minutes.

Kay would look at each passenger and ask, "Would you like a beverage?" And the passengers would look at her as if she had asked them if they would like a winning lottery ticket.

"What?" they would answer.

"Beverage?" she'd ask. "May I get you a drink?"

"What do you have?"

Instead of saying "soft drinks, juices, and milk," which is the fast answer, Kay would list every soft drink and every juice, wearing out herself and the passenger. The person she was talking to would always listen to her all the way through and then say, "I'll have a Coke."

I wondered how we were ever going to finish this service with Kay listing every beverage every time. Then I heard her lose it. Just flip out.

The poor passenger who happened to be the forty-fifth passenger to answer Kay's question with, "What do you have?" got an answer that was not according to flight attendant training.

"What do I *have?*" Kay's voice was beginning to rise, sounding a little like a car taking a corner on two wheels.

"What! Do! I! Have?!" She was definitely screeching now. *"What I have is twenty minutes to serve 170 people! Now! What do you want?!"*

"Coke," said the passenger in a small voice. "I'll have a Coke."

Kay looked at me. I looked at her. The entire plane was silent. Everyone was staring at the two wicked flight attendants, even though I was wicked only by association. "Kay," I said, waving my hand in a backward motion. "Could you go up front and get me a tea?"

Kay turned and walked into First Class, and I tried to make a joke. "She's just out of prison. You know, on a work-release program."

The lone voice of one passenger rang out: "What was she in for? Killing a passenger?"

CHAPTER 25

Peaches's Last Flight

Remember the beauty queen of my first flight? Peaches? Sadly, she didn't last long with our company. She put in her resignation after two months. She "was not a servant," she said, and "did not appreciate it" when people treated her like one. Nor did she think the constant up-and-down of the airplane was good for her legs.

I worked Peaches's last flight. My position was flight attendant in charge. Some airlines call it A-line, which simply means that I was responsible for the passengers' comfort and safety. If a passenger got into a confrontation of any sort, I'd be the one to smooth things over.

We were in the middle of a beverage service with Peaches on one end of the beverage cart and me on the other end. She served the nine passengers near her, and I served the ones near me. Suddenly I realized that Peaches was talking to a passenger who— Well, Peaches and the man had already experienced a minor run-in.

The run-in happened as I welcomed the passengers on the aircraft. Peaches was standing next to me. A man, whom we'll call Mr. Mean Passenger, rushed on at the last minute and got right up close to Peaches's face. He yelled at her, "Do you know what you did to me? You ruined my day!"

Now, Peaches had never seen this man before, but it is common for customers to blame the flight attendant in front of them for the horrible flight they just had.

"I'm sure I do not know what you mean," said Peaches.

"Your airline ruined my day! You canceled my flight, and now I'll miss my connection—"

"Well, you know," said Peaches, interrupting. "It hasn't been that great of a day for me either. I am way over due for a manicure and this humidity is just ruining my hair and—"

I jumped in. "Sir, can I help you find your seat? We're ready to go."

The man cursed and complained the whole way back to

his row. And when he got to his seat, someone else appeared to be in it. Of course it was a full flight.

"Oh, I'm so sorry," I said and asked to see each man's boarding pass. It turns out Mr. Mean Passenger was supposed to be in 28E, which was the middle seat, and Mr. Nice Passenger was seated in 28D, which was the aisle seat (and his rightful seat).

I turned to tell Mr. Mean Passenger that his seat was, in fact, the middle one. Mr. Mean Passenger started to throw a fit. "First, you mess up my whole day!" he said. "And now you want me to sit in the middle seat? Well...*you can just forget it. I'm sitting here!* " He pointed to the aisle seat that was occupied by Mr. Nice Passenger.

It was time to depart. Everyone else had boarded. Mr. Mean Passenger would not sit down, and I didn't want to delay the flight and inconvenience all the other passengers. Even taking the time to go out and get the agent could cause us to lose our takeoff time. I simply didn't know what to do. Then Mr. Nice Passenger spoke up. "Hey, you know, it's no big deal. I'll take the middle seat."

Although I had never seen Mr. Nice Passenger before, in that moment I loved him and asked Peaches to not charge him for any extras.

Now, standing at the beverage cart, Peaches asked Mr. Mean Passenger what he wanted to drink. He answered and then got angry with Peaches because we didn't carry the type of beverage he wanted. Peaches said, "Sir, I would like you to know that I am a former Miss—"

I jumped in. "Peaches, perhaps Mr. Mean Passenger would like this," and I showed him a new beverage we had just started carrying. Fortunately, that worked and Peaches moved on to get Mr. Nice Passenger, sitting in the middle, his diet beverage with a lime garnish. Only she forgot the lime. Out of the corner of my eye, I saw her suddenly stab a lime and reach over Mr. Mean Passenger's head to put the lime in Mr. Nice Passenger's drink.

Except Peaches dropped the lime right smack on top of Mr. Mean Passenger's head. It just fell off the stir stick. Quicker than you can say peaches or berries, I saw a disaster brewing. Peaches—who knew proper etiquette required never touching a lime with her fingers—grabbed a bunch of napkins, reached for the lime, and grabbed it good. So good, in fact, she ripped up not only the lime but the entire toupee that had been glued to Mr. Mean Passenger's hairless head.

For a minute time stood still as Peaches looked at the bald head beneath her and the toupee in her hand. Then she simply dropped the toupee right down into the open briefcase on Mr. Mean Passenger's lap. And turned to the next person. "Beverage? Sir? Would you like a beverage?"

There was not a sound around us as all eyes went to Mr.

Mean Passenger. Then we heard a hissing. Mr. Mean Passenger looked up at Peaches and said between clenched teeth, "I'll have your job."

"Oh, I don't think so," said Peaches. "You see, I just noticed your name tag, and you work for my daddy's corporation. And sir, I am quitting today, and I think my daddy would want to hear about your behavior."

And that was the last flight Peaches ever worked.

And an amazing flight it was, too.

CHAPTER 26

The Job Gets Difficult

All my company asked me to do was show up on time, be groomed, and be kind.

I couldn't do it. It was too much pressure.

I mean, I could do some of those things, you know, some of the time. But never, it seemed, all three in conjunction with one another. Some days I could be groomed. But not on the days I was on time. And most days I could be kind. In fact, some days I could be kind to everyone I met, every minute of being with every person—and then come home and have a kindness meltdown.

This happened to my normally quiet and soft-spoken girl-friend Karen.

Karen had just finished a three-day trip, serving hundreds of people an hour for seventeen hours of flight time. As she trudged up her front steps, using every ounce of her 105 pounds to pull her thirty-six-pound suitcase to the front door of her home, all she could think about was getting herself something to eat and drink and sitting down.

Her husband, a former football linebacker, was watching television in the living room when she came in the front door. As she walked past him to the kitchen, she heard him say, "Honey, would you bring me a drink and a—"

"The rest of his question was drowned out," she said, "by the sound of my mind snapping. I mean, it was like the kindness nerve that motivates my mouth to say nice things and my hands to do nice things just snapped.

"I imagined myself running back into the living room, fueled by some type of Post-Flight Behavior Rage. I was going to lift my husband by the shirt collar and hold him high. You know, about takeoff level, and say, *Don't you ever ask me again for anything that can be found on an airplane! Not a drink. Not a pillow. Not a blanket. Not even more ice. Do you understand? Nothing! Until I have debriefed. Are we clear? I will land you now…if we are clear.*"

She said the image of giving full vent to her anger scared

her. So, instead, she just lay down on the kitchen floor and spread her arms out like a snow angel. She just lay there until, the next thing she knew, her husband was kneeling beside her and saying, "Honey, honey, can I get you anything? Like a drink or something?"

"Oh," she said, "that would be great, but, um, what else do you have on your cart?"

Landing in the State
of Confusion

The only good part about the following story is that I was
commuting home from a trip when it happened and not
on my way to work.

Sometimes life doesn't go like we want it to. I thought
about that the first time I realized I had not only boarded the
wrong plane but had actually stayed on the plane and subsequently landed in the wrong state. I mean, I had boarded the
wrong plane before; it can happen to anyone. But I'd never

actually taken off in the wrong plane and then landed four hours later at the wrong destination.

I didn't even have a clue I was on the wrong plane until we landed. Then I poked the elbow of the passenger next to me to share a little humor over the flight attendant's mistake. "Can you believe she just announced we landed in Seattle," I snickered, "when we're in Portland, Oregon?" Tee hee.

The man looked at me as if I were an animal in a zoo.

He wasn't smiling. "We're in Seattle," he said.

"No, we're not," I said, feeling sorry for his bad case of jet lag. Then, to help him work through his obvious delusion, I continued, "I boarded a plane to Portland. I need to be in Portland. We're in Portland. Portland, Oregon."

I didn't realize at first how high the pitch of my voice was becoming. It must have sounded like the back end of an MD88 engine, whining up to take off. Only this time the flight would be from all logical thought. "We're in Portland," I screeched. "We need to be in Portland."

I don't know if you've ever experienced what happened next, but it was like one of those scary moments in a movie when the main character (me) appears very small and is looking up into distorted faces—faces that are round and huge and glaring down. It suddenly became the mission of all other passengers in the rows before me, behind me, and beside me to leer at me with news that would scare me straight.

"We're in Seattle!" they all said together, and it seemed to me that they were harmonizing in a singsong way. I was stunned.

So what could I do? I sat back down to absorb the shock. And waited for everyone to leave. Then when it was just me and the working crew left, I gathered up my bags. I said to the crew, as if in one last pitch for pity and help, "I got on the wrong plane. I mean, I thought I was going to Portland. I didn't. I went to Seattle. This is a problem."

They paused in their walk behind me and gave me the look of hatred that can only come from flight attendants to anyone holding up their crew-rest. I should have known better than to block their exit off the plane. They couldn't leave until I did. But I was simply paralyzed with frustration over what had just happened.

Get off this plane before we kill you, their look said. There was no mercy, no clemency. They wanted me gone!

I left, lugging my bags. I was now a defeated passenger who was going to get no reprieve from the airline I worked for. There are just a few things they ask of us, and one of them is to know where we are going and confirm that we are on the flight to get there. I had failed. Failed in the most basic of actions.

I felt stupid and low, and suddenly my bags seemed to weigh too much. (And I don't just mean the bags under my eyes.) I trudged down to the rental car desk and began the groveling process of begging for the lowest rate on a one-way rental—which took over an hour. Then I began the long drive from Seattle, Washington, to Portland, Oregon.

I called my husband from my cell phone in the car. "Where are you?" he said, "You should have landed an hour ago."

"I did," I said. "Just not in this state. I should be home by tomorrow morning."

"You're kidding," he said.

"No. I'm not kidding, and I don't feel like talking about it just now."

Fortunately, I was then and am now married to the most wonderful man in the world. When he heard the whole story, he started laughing and then comforted me with the words, "It could happen to anyone."

Of course it could happen to anyone. But it never would. In the history of the world, it would never happen again, but I took comfort in the fact that it could. At least in a world where someone is flying by the seat of her pants.

CHAPTER 28

Hot Towels?

I n 1989, I worked a flight with a flight attendant named Jan
who makes me laugh so much I really should never work in
the same cabin with her. Jan doesn't mean to be funny—she
just is. Even her look was funny to me. Jan was tall and thin,
but it was her hair that was especially stunning. Jan liked puff,
so she doubled the size of her long, dark tresses with hair exten-
sions. Here was this tall, thin flight attendant with a winning
smile and huge hair.

The flight was a long one, over three hours, and Jan and I
were assigned to First Class. This was in the days when First

Class included a four-course meal, served on china, with silver and linens on the table and hot towels distributed before dinner. My favorite presentation was the hot towels—passengers loved getting the personal warm towels to clean their face and hands.

As we prepared the hot towels, I mentioned to Jan that I liked to do the dry-ice presentation with the towels. She had never heard this secret to making the hot towels look extra steamy. So I showed her.

I arranged the hot towels in a circle and poured the steaming water over them. Then, for extra effect, I put a small piece of dry ice in a cup of water in the center. Adding water to dry ice results in a lovely cloud of white smoke curling up around the towels.

I soon learned that Jan's rule in life is, "If a little is good, more is better," and that rule didn't apply just to her hair. I left the galley after I showed her how to set up the hot towels, and I was standing in the back of the cabin when she came out with her presentation. I was dumbstruck.

She hadn't used the small tray I had suggested. She had used the largest tray we had. And she hadn't used just one piece of dry ice in a tiny cup. She had used every piece of dry ice on the plane in a huge pile in the middle. A mountain of dry ice. She had poured so much water on the dry ice that it looked as if she were walking in a volcano of smoke. From her waist to her head, you saw smoke. Billowing white circles of smoke.

Apparently Jan realized she couldn't see well enough to walk. So she took the metal tongs and used the tongs to wave one of the towels in what appeared to be a serious effort to clear the smoke in front of her. The effort wasn't working.

What the passengers saw was a torso with legs surrounded at the top by a swirl of white smoke, with glimpses of dark hair wherever Jan waved the towel. Huge dark hair.

As she moved forward, no one spoke except Jan.

"Hot towel?" she said. "Hot towel?"

One passenger, a woman in the front row, finally looked up as Jan approached and then leaned over and pulled out a tiny personal fan, which she pointed in the direction of the hot towels. When the smoke parted, the woman grabbed a hot towel, saying, "Delighted, I'm sure."

After that I hid the dry ice from Jan.

CHAPTER 29

Dreams of Sleeping
in the Ice Bucket

It seemed like a good trip in the beginning. The reason I chose to work it is that the first night's layover included twenty hours at Daytona Beach, Florida, in a hotel right on the beach. My husband agreed to drive the four-hour trip from our home in Savannah, Georgia, with our seven-year-old daughter, Mandy. We would all stay in a fine hotel, eat at fine restaurants, and play at the beach.

Everything went as planned. Tom, Mandy, and I had a

great twenty hours at the beach making a memorable home movie. Mandy later said it was the best movie she ever saw.

The second day of the trip looked easier than the first. I would simply fly two easy legs: Daytona to Atlanta, then Atlanta to Newark, New Jersey. What could go wrong?

The first thing that went wrong was that after a night and all day at the beach with my family, I was tired. On the Daytona Beach to Atlanta trip, we flew in the early evening, and I had difficulty staying awake. Next, my allergies were acting up. When I couldn't find my allergy medicine, in desperation (I mean I can't work with a drippy nose) I took an over-the-counter sleeping pill that contained an antihistamine, thinking I'd be in the hotel room in Newark in less than two hours before the I'm-drugged-and-can't-stay-awake feeling hit me.

I took the tablet at 9:30 p.m. Our flight was due to take off at 9:43 p.m.

Our pilots were late arriving in Atlanta, delaying our take-off a bit. Then, just as the pilots announced we were ready for pushback, a flash of lightning lit the sky near our aircraft. All takeoff times were delayed, and an hour later, the airport was shut down. Here I was—barely conscious—on the airplane with all the passengers, sitting at the gate for two hours. Finally at 11:30 p.m., we took off. I have very little memory of that flight. My coworker said she couldn't believe how awake I seemed. And that I appeared to function normally.

But in reality, I faked staying awake. For weeks after that trip, I had a recurring nightmare in which I was draped over one end of the beverage cart with my face down in the ice: my eyes were open, but I was sound asleep. In my dream, my coworker pushed me along, saying to the passengers, "Beverages? Beverages? Oh, don't mind the sleeping flight attendant. We'll use a different bucket of ice for your drink. Beverages? Beverages?"

I have never again substituted over-the-counter sleep aids for allergy medicine. You just never know when the flight will be delayed several hours and you'll be tempted to use an ice bucket for a pillow.

CHAPTER 30

Sleeping in the Closet

I was on my way from Seattle, Washington, to Atlanta, Georgia, and there were no seats on the airplane. So I had to fly "jump seat." Jump-seat riding is what flight attendants do when there are no passenger seats but they want to travel so bad they are willing to sit on a hard little seat that is virtually unpadded and meant to harness crew for takeoffs and landings.

Only trained flight crew are allowed to fly jump seat. It is not comfortable, but it does get you where you are going. We can be in street clothes on the jump seat, but we have to have our IDs out and available. On this trip, the captain turned off the seat-belt sign and left it off. As soon as the sign went off, I talked to the flight attendant in charge, whom I knew, and mentioned how tired I was. I told her about flying all night the night before and spending the day running around visiting friends. And how difficult it was going to be sitting up on a jump seat all night. "Well," she said, jokingly, "there is no one in the closet."

I looked in the extra luggage closet. It was three feet deep and nineteen inches wide, and I thought, *I can fit in here.* I got in, spread a blanket on the floor, and slept soundly for the three hours and eighteen minutes until descent.

So, if you were one of the passengers on the flight that day who went to use the First Class bathroom but opened the wrong door instead, it was me you saw. Me on the floor, using my coat for a pillow, sleeping in the closet.

Chapter 31

Stupid Dad Tricks

Sometimes when my family wants to get away for a mini-vacation, Tom will ask me to look for a trip that has a long layover and open flights, and Tom and Mandy will come with me. Last summer I found just such a trip—a thirty-hour layover in Springfield, Massachusetts. It was on that trip that Tom did what he now refers to as a Stupid Dad Trick.

It wasn't that Tom meant to do anything that would be classified as not smart. He had only the best intentions in mind as he tried to teach our seven-year-old daughter, Mandy, to do backward flips into the hotel pool. Tom later said he didn't notice the sharp aluminum edging around the pool or how far the concrete gutters stuck out into the water.

As a testament to Tom's teaching ability—or Mandy's learning ability—she did get a lot of height on her spin. And flip. In fact, she was completely upside down when she crashed. Which would have been good if she'd been over water. She wasn't.

She hit the side of the pool with the top of her head, slicing a straight line across the top of her skull. As she continued down, now propelled to the edge of the water, her forehead slammed into the concrete edging.

Let me tell you right now, Mandy survived with no brain damage. And no permanent scarring, except for the scar across the top of her skull, which is mostly hidden by her hair.

As we describe the accident now to friends and family who weren't there to watch, we like to say, "She didn't bleed that much. They only had to drain the pool twice."

We actually don't know how many times they drained the pool because, as soon Tom saw the cut on the top of Mandy's head and the blood running down her face, he raced her upstairs to the room, where I was quietly writing another chapter about our chaotic life. He needed my help in deciding what hospital in this unfamiliar city would be best to stitch up the gash in a seven-year-old's head.

Later that evening, when everything was calm, Tom mournfully said, "I'm so sorry. I feel terrible."

"It was an accident," I said. "It could have happened to anyone."

"You would never have allowed her to jump backward off a hotel pool," he said. "It was a Stupid Dad Trick."

I wanted to say, "You're right on the first and second points," but since I've done a few well-meaning dumb things myself, I was in no place to judge. So I just said, "Thank God it wasn't worse. I mean, she could have broken her neck or her nose or had brain damage."

On my next trip as a flight attendant, I was still so stunned by the accident—more stunned by what could have happened and didn't—that I felt the need to talk about the incident. I told the flight attendant sitting with me in the back of the plane the whole story.

"Oh, that's nothing," she said. "Listen to what my husband did on his Stupid Dad Trick day."

Apparently she had been on a long layover at a Miami hotel, and her husband had come to visit her and brought their three-month-old daughter. Mom was in the room resting, and Dad decided to take Baby to the pool. Not wanting Baby to get any sun damage, the Dad had greased her all over with a thick coating of SPF 45 sunscreen. Then they got in the pool. That's when Dad realized Baby was slippery. So slippery that she popped out of his grip, and when he tried to capture her, he couldn't.

"It was like trying to catch a greased watermelon," he said. Dad said he tried at least ten times, each time more desperate than the others, to grab hold of that baby. He estimates she was underwater for several seconds, maybe even a full minute, before he finally got a grip on her diaper and lifted her out of the water. He said the baby was laughing and happy as could be.

But the dad was so shaken by the incident that it was five years before he told his wife about it. "You would have strung me up by my thumbs," he said. "It was a Stupid Dad Trick, but I was just trying to do the right thing."

I like to think that kids have special baby angels that protect them from things like Stupid Dad Tricks. And keep their well-meaning dads from having to deal with what might have happened.

CHAPTER 32

Passenger Gone Wild

I was working a full flight on a L1011—and I mean completely full. I was serving beverages in the aisle when a passenger, who seemed upset, tapped me on the shoulder. He was distinguished looking and spoke with grace and aplomb. "Excuse me," he said, "do you have any empty seats? The woman next to me is, well, it would be best if I could relocate."

"We don't," I said. "I'm sorry." I always feel bad when someone pays what is comparable to a down payment on a new car to fly somewhere, only to find that the person in the next seat is rude or smells or is a talker. I didn't know what the woman next to him was like, but the truth was that every seat was full—we had left ticketed passengers standing at the gate.

About ten minutes later, the same man approached me again. Although still reserved and very polite, he was obviously becoming desperate.

"The woman next to me," he said, motioning to his section of the aircraft. "She's a bit difficult. Do you have *any* empty seats?"

"No, I'm sorry, we don't."

It wasn't until the third time the man returned that I realized the gravity of the situation.

"Excuse me," he said. "She bit me."

"*What?*"

"She bit me, yes. Here on the arm."

He held up his arm and showed a fresh imprint of a set of teeth. I looked up at the other flight attendant who had heard the whole thing. And then we went into action. We called the cockpit. The second officer came out and subdued the woman using a rope of headset cords tied together to secure her arms to her side, and we removed all passengers within teeth range.

We had to double up people in seats, and we immediately diverted the aircraft to land at the closest available airport. The cockpit called ahead for someone to meet the flight. So when we landed police were at the door and stormed onto the airplane while all the passengers who had been instructed to stay seated did so.

The biter was escorted off the flight, and the bitten received a free beverage.

In an update later in the day, we heard the biter was a former mental patient who had simply forgotten to take her medicine.

When we took off again this time, we did have one empty seat.

CHAPTER 33

The Strangest Thing That Happened on My Flight

The year was 1986, and I was working the dreaded Los Angeles to Las Vegas turns: six flights a day, up and down, racing through the cabin with drinks during the thirty-seven-minute trip.

Now, in those days, the airline allowed smoking on board. And smoking mixed with all the drinking that went on during the Las Vegas runs was a dangerous combination.

That's why when the woman sitting in the last row of First

Class, seat 3A, called me over and pointed below the window and said with slurred speech, "I've dropped my cigarette, and it's stuck on the wall," I went into action. I leaned over the man sitting next to her and saw that her cigarette was indeed stuck in the carpeting on the wall. Smoke drifted up as the cigarette's embers burned the carpet fibers.

As I was trained to do, I grabbed the water off the woman's tray and poured it over the side toward the cigarette. The water bounced off the curve in the wall and missed the fire altogether.

I notified another crew member to alert the cockpit. Then I took a fire extinguisher and asked the other two people in First Class to leave their seats while I tried to extinguish the flame from the cabin. That way no one in Coach would see what I was doing and be alarmed. But it didn't work. I needed a different angle.

So, holding the extinguisher down near my knees—which I hoped was out of sight of most people—I quickly stepped beyond the curtain into Coach. I said, "Excuse me," to the people in A, B, and C seats as I knelt. Having a clear shot at the tiny fire along the side wall under the windows, I sprayed the extinguisher until it was empty. It completely eliminated any hint of flame. Sweat had formed on my forehead from the pressure, and I was standing up to go back to First Class when I heard a call bell.

I looked up to see the woman sitting one row back in the

aisle seat motioning me over. She had apparently been watching everything I did, and now she had a comment. She was, it turned out, quite disgusted with my behavior. She tapped large red nails on the tray table.

"Yes?" I said. "Can I help you?"

"I don't think now is a good time to spray for bugs," she said, waving a finger at me.

"Excuse me?"

"I don't think now is a good time to spray for bugs! I can see you're trying to hide that, and you're not fooling me one bit." She pointed at the cylinder I tried to hide behind my legs.

A couple of seconds passed while I thought about her statement. Then I said, "You're absolutely right. I'm going to put this away right now."

And I did.

Sometimes it's best to go down the path with those who think they know where you are going.

CHAPTER 34

Suzy New Hire

She was a young flight attendant—*young* meaning just twenty-two years old. I was someone who had been working for twenty years and felt a hundred years old. It was an all-night turnaround. Atlanta to Los Angeles and back again. The flight attendants would have no break between flights. It was board, take off, deplane, clean plane, reboard, and take off again.

By around 4:45 a.m. on the way back to Atlanta, the entire plane was sleeping, except for the flight attendants, who were mostly going about their duties quietly. Except for the young one, Suzy New Hire. She was spinning out of control with excitement about the job and her life and her new boyfriend and her old boyfriend and where she was going on vacation and what she was going to fix for dinner when she got back home. Just listening to the speed with which words tumbled out of her mouth made me tired.

I realized that Suzy New Hire had been getting progressively more talkative after midnight. As I looked at her in my exhausted state, she reminded me of a helicopter with the blades spinning at full speed.

I, on the other hand, felt like an old jet with my wings drooping near the ground.

But suddenly I realized she was saying something I wanted to remember. So I wrote it down.

She was talking with another flight attendant and stopped midsentence. "Ew," she said. "Ewww. That was so just, like, you know, Taj Mahal."

"What?" said the other flight attendant.

"Taj Mahal." That was *Ewww. Taj Mal.*

Then she paused and said, "Or is that *déjà vu?*"

CHAPTER 35

Little Hannah Gray

I never stay in touch with passengers after a flight. Despite the fact that during a flight we may bond and they may share some of their deepest secrets with me—as passengers are wont to do because they know they will never see me again. And despite the fact that I may tell them I love them (by which, I mean, the passenger is my new best friend at the moment), I basically know I'll never see most of them or hear from most of them again.

Frankly, one of the joys of my job is the love 'em and leave 'em factor. Hopefully, I leave 'em laughing, but once the flight is over, so is the relationship.

The need for this "leave 'em for good" approach is simply logistics. On a busy day, I might come in contact with a thousand people a day. Five flights, two hundred people each flight. If I were to work just two and a half days a week, that's ten thousand people a month. Keeping tabs on every relationship I form would be impossible.

But there was one little passenger I will never forget. In fact, I dedicated my first book to her. Her name is Hannah Gray. A lot of people who read that dedication ask me questions about Hannah. Here are the answers to those questions:

- I met Hannah when she was ten years old. We talked on the flight and then stayed in touch via e-mail for years. In the beginning of our e-mailing, Hannah's mother wrote to me and (understandably) asked, *Why are you e-mailing my daughter?* I wrote back to her mother and invited her to read every e-mail I sent to Hannah. I wrote, *I am e-mailing your daughter because she is delightful and creative and funny, and I see in her what I dream of one day having in a child of my own.*

- When she was thirteen or fourteen, Hannah e-mailed me about what it was like when kids at school thought she was retarded because of her cerebral palsy. And later she wrote of potential boyfriends and career dreams and new best friends.

- Hannah heard that Tom and I prayed for a baby, and I told her, "If I ever have a daughter, I want her to be just like you."

- When our daughter, Mandy, was finally born, I would have named her Hannah, but most of our friends used that name, and I didn't want six Hannahs in our neighborhood.

- When Hannah Gray got word of Mandy's birth, she sent us a present. It was a gift she had made in wood-shop—a wooden name-tag for Mandy's door with each letter of her name carved out—no small feat for a person with cerebral palsy. Mandy recently turned eight years old. We still have Hannah's gift. We still cherish it.

- How many years did I stay in touch with Hannah Gray? I lost count, but I met her when she was ten, and when we e-mailed last, she was in college.

- Did Hannah ever read my first book? Yes, I sent her the book when it came out, and she wrote back via e-mail and said she liked the stories.

- Did I ever see Hannah again after that first flight? No. I just dedicated my first book to her, e-mailed her, and one day want to tell my daughter about her courage and grace.

- Have I communicated further with Hannah's parents? Yes, I once sent her mother a couple of e-mails telling her she had a wonderful daughter. And when Hannah was a teenager and entered a hospital to essentially have her legs cut off and sewn back on so she could walk without the aid of a walker or wheelchair, I sent flowers and a note to her in the hospital. For the first time, I heard from her father. He wrote, "Thank you. Thank you for being so nice to my daughter."

- Do I still think of Hannah? Yes, of course. You can't forget someone like Hannah Gray. My family still has the first picture Hannah ever sent us. It's of her as a ten-year-old, and it holds the highest place of honor in our home. It is displayed on our refrigerator door.

Hannah falls into the category of rare people you meet for a moment who affect your life forever.

CHAPTER 36

Wally—Who Was Eighty-Seven Years Old

Wally was eighty-seven years old the day he boarded. I know because he told me.

The gate agent introduced us and handed me Wally's arm. "Wally might need a bit of extra care," he said.

Wally had a difficult time walking, but eventually we made it to his seat.

As I took care of getting him fastened in the seat belt and showing him where the bathroom was, Wally seemed upset.

The agent turned and left, Wally grabbed my hand and drew me to him and said in a broken voice, "They took away my license today. They took away my driver's license."

I listened to him and realized this must have been Wally's last claim to independence—his ability to drive himself when and where he wanted. It was obvious that he was devastated.

I knelt beside him and looked him right in the eye. "Oh, Wally," I said, "I am so sorry."

"They took away my license," he said, his eyes filled with tears.

I stayed for just a minute more. Then I had to help board our 120 passengers. We got everyone on board, and during my last cabin walk-through before takeoff, Wally grabbed my arm again. "They took away my license," he said, with an earnestness that made me wish I could get that bit of independence back for him.

I knelt by him again and said the only thing I could. "I am so sorry, Wally. That must be awful for you."

It was a busy flight, but I was able to kneel beside Wally's seat three more times to offer a bit of empathy. And each time I stopped to be with Wally, I realized anew that this is the greatest calling in the world—just to be kind to someone, to offer a cup of compassion in the name of love.

It's been eight years since I had that flight with Wally, and I still think of him, still wonder how he fared.

CHAPTER 37

Meeting Erma Bombeck

When I was young, still living at home with my three siblings and a mom who was desperate to find a little humor in our household, we borrowed books by Erma Bombeck from our library.

I never dreamed I would actually meet Erma. I did dream about winning a Pulitzer Prize, but seeing Erma Bombeck in person would be akin to a Catholic meeting the Pope or a Southern Baptist meeting Billy Graham. It would be like a miracle, something only God could arrange.

One day, before my first book was published but after some of my humor articles had garnered praise, I was working on a flight where I was assigned to Coach but was in First Class for takeoff and landing. After boarding, I strapped in, and as the plane roared down the runway, I absent-mindedly glanced up at the faces of the First-Class passengers.

Suddenly, I grabbed my shoulder straps to keep from falling over in shock. *It couldn't be. It absolutely could not be true.* I ripped the passenger manifest from the hands of the other flight attendant and looked at the names for Row 3, Seats C and D. I could hardly believe they would travel under their real names: Bombeck, Erma and Bill.

I screamed silently to get my mom's attention in heaven. *"Take a look at this!"* I told her.

As soon as the seat-belt sign went off, I stood up and ran to Erma's seat to pounce on her like the rabid fan I was, but alas, she and Bill were sound asleep. I later learned they were traveling home from China, and they'd boarded our plane in Atlanta for their last short hop. They were exhausted.

There was nothing for me to do but go work in Coach the rest of the flight. I hoped there would be time to speak to Erma before the end of the flight—or at least that she'd be awake by then. I was desperate to talk to her. I wanted to tell her how much she meant to me. I wanted to tell her that in all my years of growing up, she had been the one person who taught me the healing power of a humorous story—of laughing at the things that happen to us.

I wanted to tell her so much. But I couldn't wake her up to tell her that. So, after the beverage service (because she was still asleep), I sat on the First-Class jump seat and watched her like a falcon watches its prey, waiting for a good time to pounce. Throughout the entire flight, she never did wake up. So I wrote a note that I would give her as she walked off the airplane.

Dear Erma,

When I was a little girl in a big family, and there was not much fun in our household, my mom and I would take refuge in your books. We would read the chapters to each other as we did dishes or fixed meals. We laughed, and sometimes cried, as we found a kindred spirit in you.

Erma, I have started getting my own humorous inspirational essays published. And have just been offered a contract for my first book. Your legacy lives on, Erma, in writers like me who were inspired by you. I just want you to know that.

Love, Marsha Marks

Finally, during the last minute on final approach, Erma woke up. I was by her side in a flash. I handed her her coat and knelt by her seat. "Erma," I said, getting choked up, "I've always admired you." And I gave her the note. She read it, and then in true Erma fashion woke up her husband to show it to him.

I watched them both read it, and I heard Erma say, "Look, Bill, isn't this neat?" And the joy of the moment was not lost on me as I looked up and said to my mom, who I hoped was paying attention, *"Did you see that? Can you believe that?"*

We have had lots of celebrities on board, some more famous and some more wealthy, but none more honored, in my own mind, than the great (now late) Erma Bombeck.

CHAPTER 38

Sandra Bullock, NBC, and Me

S o you've read this whole book and now you're thinking, *What else? Are there any more adventures in the works? I mean, we got the flying career, the husband, the kid and a few books published. Let's move on.*

Well, I am moving on. The new plan involves Sandra Bullock, NBC, and me. I need to tell you at this time that I have never met Sandra Bullock, but I do have a plan to meet her. The plan is this: I've heard she loves to eat at this restaurant that is only one hour from my home. So I go there, sit, and eat, and try to look like I'm a resident of that community. I do it all the time. One day (in my version of this dream), she will walk in, see me alone (less threatening), notice my official-looking NBC ID tag, and assume I'm in "the business."

The truth is, I'm not in the business. I don't know one person from NBC and wouldn't know an entertainment executive if I ran into one. In fact, I still have my day job. I am still a flight attendant. Serving beverages and saving lives…mostly serving beverages.

Which explains how I got the NBC luggage tag in the first place. I bought it at the NBC store while on a layover in New York. You can buy NBC mugs, T-shirts, and luggage tags. My husband said the luggage tag looks cheesy. But at least it has the NBC colors and the peacock, and it has been the segue to some cool conversations with people who see the NBC luggage tag and assume I'm someone more important to them than a flight attendant.

I must at this time tell you how I know people notice the NBC tag and treat me differently because of it. In 1999 I was attending a big writers' conference that I could not afford to attend. I had just purchased the NBC luggage tags and forgotten they were even on my bags. I got off the plane, put on my sunglasses, adjusted my sun hat, and was immediately stalked by this nice guy, who identified himself as also attending the "big conference"—and who seemed to have a great desire to carry my luggage.

I couldn't believe it. I asked him what he did, and he said he had won some screenplay competition in Sun Valley, Idaho, and had a new screenplay entered in the competition here.

"That is so cool," I said. I was too intimidated to say I had never entered a contest in my life, had never written a screenplay, and at that time, didn't have any books published.

"Yes," he said respectfully, as if he were talking to someone who could affect his career—in a big way. Then he paused, waiting for me to speak.

I didn't speak. I was pondering why he had such a solicitous attitude. And just when I had decided it was because he was genuinely a nice person, he spoke again. "You work for NBC?"

The question struck me as weird, completely absurd.

"*What?*" I said.

"For NBC?" he said and pointed to my luggage tags.

I doubled over in laughter. "No," I said. "Honestly…I'm a flight attendant. I just bought those tags at the NBC store in New York."

He dropped my bags so fast I tripped over them. And then he left. My first taste of Hollywood.

I began to schlep my own luggage and ponder the shallowness of people who treat people they think can help them with respect and people they deem unable to help them with disdain. The whole incident had deep psychological and spiritual ramifications, but mostly it was just funny.

For a long time after that, I didn't use those luggage tags. They were buried in one of our many boxes from our three moves in the past two years. But I recently discovered them again, and now you're getting the picture of how I think this Sandra Bullock thing could play out.

My dear husband, who is, as I've mentioned, from Lincoln, Nebraska, would like me to insert here that the behavior I have described in this chapter is, "Soooo *not* Midwest behavior." He does not mean this remark as a compliment. He means it as a caution. In fact, I had to make a pact with him that I would not do anything weird like sitting for hours in this restaurant where Sandra Bullock has been sighted. (Like no one else has ever done that at a celebrity hangout.)

To keep peace in our family, I had to agree to some basic legal-type rules: at no time will I resort to putting anything— a screenplay, for example—in Sandra Bullock's mailbox, which I think is some sort of federal offense. But, if I had the screenplay finished (I mean written someplace other than in my mind), I'd be tempted to leave a screenplay sitting on the table of her favorite restaurant with her name on it, official-looking. I bet someone would get it to her. Hold on—I'm not going to do that. I'm only explaining a temptation here.

Also, Tom asked me to promise that at no time will I even

try to follow her car or anything like that: we're talking staking not stalking. Tom said I had to promise this last thing after one day I simply asked him to drive around the area where she is said to own a home…for eight hours or so. He drove for eight minutes. When we didn't see her car, he insisted on driving home. But, I said, what if she had some sign up in her lawn that said, *Marsha, I know you're looking for me, and I want the screenplay.* That, I think, would be a sign from God.

I actually don't even know where she lives, but if I did, I'd be walking up and down in front of her house with my script in hand and my NBC tag in plain view. Carrying groceries or something so it looked like I lived in the neighborhood and just happened to have my script with me. *Hey, wise as a serpent.*

My husband didn't need to tell me those rules. I want to be creative in my approach, not weird.

This is how I imagine this latest scene of hanging out here at Sandra Bullock's favorite restaurant playing out: I don't even plan on speaking to Sandra first. She will speak to me. It's cooler to let them be interested in you.

I'll be sitting here in her favorite hangout, typing on my laptop. On the table in plain view will be what looks like a finished script, and in even plainer view will be my NBC tag, and she will walk up to me and say, "So you're working on a *feature?*" (And I'll know what she means.)

Then as I try not to pass out because my dream is coming

true, I'll casually tell her the truth. "Sandy," I'll say (I'm sure her friends call her Sandy), "I've got the funniest movie for you."

She will love it. And the reason she will is that she plays me, someone who can be a funny nut. Sandra is good with funny nut-type characters.

It isn't that I ever dreamed of being a funny nut. In fact, I take myself quite seriously. It's just that I seem to end up in situations that cause people to ask me if I'm nuts. And then, when the situations work out, people seem to be shocked. You want some examples? I just gave you a whole book of them.

But just so you can be on the inside of this deal with me, I'll tell you the opening lines to the screenplay. First the setting:

A little girl (me as a kid) has locked herself into a tiny bathroom in a small apartment, and she is singing, "Make me a blessing, make me a blessing, out of my life may Jesus shine. Make me a blessing, O Savior, I pray. Make me a blessing to someone today."

And then her Uncle Louie, played by Danny DeVito, pounds on the bathroom door and says, "If you don't get outta there and let me use the john, there's gonna be some blessing going on."

And then the rest of the movie will be stories in this book and from, you know, other books and future books.

And now I'm done, hoping that I've left you wanting more. You have to leave them wanting more. Always wanting more. Because my life's motto, which I have waited till now to tell you, is, "Only in heaven is fullness of joy. On earth we are always left wanting…wanting more."

So, I hope I meet you one day on some adventure, when I'm flying by the seat of my pants.

Afterword

W*here are they now?* I promised to tell you what each of the flight attendants mentioned in the dedication is doing now. Here they are:

TRACY (MANKE) FRAME was only a flight attendant for a very short time, as her daddy owns a large business (Manke Lumber) in the Pacific Northwest and it was agreed that she would fly only until she got married. She has always been drop-dead beautiful, and she went on to become Mrs. Deward William Frame III. She is the mother of three children and spends her days playing tennis, volunteering with the Junior League, and attending social events. She remains to this day one of my most cherished friends.

SUSAN (HEAD) EVANS is the flight attendant I wrote about in my book *101 Simple Lessons for Life*. And also referred to in my book *If I Ignore It, It Will Go Away...and Other Lies I Thought Were True.* After Susan lost a child (her second baby, named Jack) to sudden infant death syndrome, she took ten years leave from flying and to this date has never returned. She spends her days as the mother of three children and maintains a lovely home, which was listed in *Better Homes and Gardens* as

"Today's English Tudor." (I love telling people that.) She and I and Tracy Frame meet at least once a year for wing-sister lunches. Susan Evans and Tracy Frame are the two flight attendants in my life whom I have spent the most time with outside of work.

SALLY (BLACKIE) BARTLETT is now living in Southern California. She is happily married and the mother of one little boy. She works part time as a personal trainer at an exclusive health club. And she has recently begun a successful career as a writer. Of all my flight attendant girlfriends, Sally and I were most often together on international layovers. We ate McDonald's in Seoul, Korea, ate pastries near the Eiffel Tower in Paris, had tea in London, and have remained in touch for more than twenty years. I still consider her one of my closest friends.

MELANIE FEDDERSEN is also one of my closest wing-sisters who hasn't flown in more than ten years. She shared a home with me during the early years of my career and is the only one of my former wing-sisters who has not yet found Mr. Right. She is a very successful corporate real estate agent in Chicago and the mother of a two-year-old. You may e-mail her at ivybysea@aol.com but only if you have the perfect man for her. (Think of me as her matchmaker. She tells me she is happily single, but as her matchmaker I know she really means, "No bizarre dates, please.")

You may also e-mail her if you want a luxury property in

Chicago. She is blonde, five foot three, and wears a size 4. (I'm almost over hating her for this.) My favorite recent Melanie story happened when I visited her this year in Chicago. She had to show a home to a movie-star client. She wasn't allowed to disclose the name of the movie star. And due to my propensity to go nuts when around celebrities, she made me wait in the car. With the windows rolled up. Across the street. Well, was it my fault that I watched her every move with binoculars? When I saw John Cusack ride up on his bike and act normal while he met her, I started screaming so loud, she said they could hear me despite the fact that the windows were rolled up. She later mentioned I was also clawing at the window. She said she glanced over at me and frowned, as if to say, "I have no idea who that is." And then she walked into the secure building with John. (Now listen, John Cusack, if you are reading this, there is a part for you and Joan in the movie. E-mail me at marshamarks@aol.com, and we'll talk about it.)

Flight attendant Melanie Capado, who is not mentioned in the dedication, recently sent word to me through Susan Evans that I once told her I would mention her in a book. Here is that mention: I used to fly with Melanie out of Seattle and have never in my life met a flight attendant who reminded me more of a movie star. So, Sandra Bullock, if you're reading this, we have to put Melanie in the movie too! Sorry, that is just my demand. (Unless you don't want to.)

Acknowledgments

First acknowledgments for this book go to my three early readers, all of whom I called every five minutes for five months straight to read them a comment or comment on an edit. They are (in order of how often they were called):

1. Connie Smiley, an artist and my friend for thirty years.

2. Christy Award–winning novelist Michael Morris. If you want to know how I met Michael Morris, read my first book, *101 Amazing Things About God.* It's a great story that continues to this day.

3. Author Sue Farren. Watch for her 2005 release from Hyperion. Sue was recently written up in the *Wall Street Journal* for innovation in selling her book to Hyperion. She has been a friend for two years.

I am blessed personally and professionally to know these people and to have their private phone numbers.

Thanks to Chris Ferebee (attorney) at Yates and Yates for negotiating my first four book contracts and thereby changing my life—and helping dreams come true. Thanks to Sealy Yates for still acting like he knows me in public when I've been such an "odd" client. And to Susan Yates and Curtis Yates for still laughing after all these years.

Thanks to Elisa Fryling Stanford and Don Pape (my first editor on this project and my revered publisher, respectively). And thanks to Shannon Hill (the final editor) who, in the eleventh hour, had to receive a Hail Mary pass of this manuscript and managed to carry it across the finish line...so the team looked good.

Thanks to Joel Kneedler and the whole WaterBrook publicity and marketing team for helping me to understand that it isn't just about writing a book; it's about getting the word out. And to Brian, head of sales, who told me, "This time, write a book about being a flight attendant."

Thanks to the people who run these restaurants where I sat for hours and wrote this book: The Breakfast Club in Tybee Island, Georgia; Baibry's Café and Frank and Linda's Café in Rincon, Georgia; and Truffles in Bluffton, South Carolina.

Also, thanks to Tom and Mandy (my husband and daughter) who prayed every day near the end of this book that I would just finish it! And their prayers were answered finally... with yes.

About the Author

Marsha Marks is a popular speaker and author known for her ability to blend humor with spiritual insights. She is the author of *101 Amazing Things About God, 101 Simple Lessons for Life,* and *If I Ignore It, It Will Go Away.* She is also a former contributing editor to *Campus Life.*

Her articles and stories have appeared in such publications as *Writer's Digest, Eternity, Moody Monthly,* and *The Christian Reader,* and she has appeared on numerous radio and television programs, including *Life Today* with James and Betty Robison. Marsha and her family make their home in Savannah, Georgia.

Please visit Marsha at www.flyingbytheseatofmypants.net, or write to her at marshamarks@aol.com.

"This book will make you laugh, cheer, and ponder God's grace in a new light."

—MICHAEL MORRIS, author of *A Place Called Wiregrass*

"Marsha Marks shows us how to take faith seriously and life with a sense of humor."

—LAURIE BETH JONES, author of *Jesus CEO* and *Teach Your Team to Fish*

Through real-life stories, thoughful reflections, and hilarious honesty, Marsha Marks reveals life-affirming truths about everyday life.

Available in bookstores everywhere.

WATERBROOK PRESS

www.waterbrookmultnomah.com

To learn more about WaterBrook Press and view
our catalog of products, log on to our Web site:
www.waterbrookpress.com

WATERBROOK
PRESS

Printed in the United States
by Baker & Taylor Publisher Services